Jim Molan is an Australian Liberal senator and retired army major general. He has been an infantryman, a helicopter pilot, a commander of army units (from a 30-man platoon to a division of 15,000 soldiers), commander of the Australian Defence Colleges, and commander of the evacuation force from the Solomon Islands in 2000. He has served in Papua New Guinea, Indonesia, East Timor, Malaysia, Germany, the US and Iraq.

In April 2004, he deployed for a year to Iraq as the Coalition forces' chief of operations, where he controlled the manoeuvre operations of all forces across Iraq, including maintaining the security of Iraq's oil, electricity and rail infrastructure. Described as 'the ADF member most directly involved in fighting the insurgents', he was awarded the Distinguished Service Cross by the Australian government for 'distinguished command and leadership in action in Iraq', and the Legion of Merit by the US Government.

Since leaving the military, Jim has been a commentator on defence and security issues and has written regularly for a number of journals and blogs. He was part owner of an Australian company facilitating access for Australian industry to defence technology grants and working with other high-tech industries, and he was nominated as chairman of two companies attempting to commence trading in Australia. He was a consultant to Deakin University, BAE Systems Australia, and Israeli Aerospace Industries.

As well as being involved in formulating the Coalition's defence policy while in opposition (2012–13), Jim was a co-author, with Scott Morrison MP, of the Coalition policy on border control. Following the 2013 federal election, Jim was appointed to the full-time position of Prime Minister's Special Envoy for Operation Sovereign Borders. He has been active in speaking out on defence issues, particularly Australia's preparedness against an aggressive China. He lives on a property outside Canberra.

JIM MOLAN

DANGER ON OUR DOORSTEP

HarperCollins*Publishers*

HarperCollins*Publishers*
Australia • Brazil • Canada • France • Germany • Holland • India
Italy • Japan • Mexico • New Zealand • Poland • Spain • Sweden
Switzerland • United Kingdom • United States of America

HarperCollins acknowledges the Traditional Custodians of the land upon
which we live and work, and pays respect to Elders past and present.

First published in Australia in 2022
by HarperCollins*Publishers* Australia Pty Limited
Gadigal Country
Level 13, 201 Elizabeth Street, Sydney NSW 2000
ABN 36 009 913 517
harpercollins.com.au

A catalogue record for this book is available from the National Library of Australia

ISBN 978 1 4607 6260 8 (paperback)
ISBN 978 1 4607 1522 2 (ebook)

Cover design by George Saad
Cover image by Clem Onojeghuo on Unsplash; soldier silhouette by shutterstock.com
Maps by Map Illustrations, www.mapillustrations.com.au
Typeset in Sabon LT Std by Kirby Jones
Printed and bound in Australia by McPherson's Printing Group

To my children, Sarah, Erin, Felicity and Michael, and my grandchildren, Sophie, Angus, Eliza, Grace and Andrew, with love and in the hope that your Australia will remain 'one and free', and also sovereign, safe and prosperous.

CONTENTS

FOREWORD

by Peter Dutton, Minister for Defence

It is a pleasure to write this foreword to *Danger on Our Doorstep*. Although I'd been aware of Jim Molan for quite some time, I first got to know him well during the Rudd–Gillard–Rudd government of 2006–13. We were in opposition. After we assumed government, against all professional advice and media commentary, and working with Immigration Minister Scott Morrison, Jim provided the means whereby a simple political policy of 'Stop the Boats' was converted into the strategy that became 'Operation Sovereign Borders'. This was no easy accomplishment. The Rudd and Gillard governments had proved over six years how difficult it was to make such a conversion, and not one public voice was of the opinion that it was possible. The combination of Scott Morrison and Jim Molan was most effective, not just in formulating policy and strategy, but also in explaining the policy and then making it work in government.

Jim has brought the same insight to the Parliamentary Joint Committee on Intelligence and Security (PJCIS). Again, he's been ahead of his time, arguing for the formation of the Home Affairs portfolio. Jim was proved right.

Danger on Our Doorstep is a serious work by Jim Molan. It is a manifestation of all Jim's qualities. With clarity, Jim deals with some of the most complex and sensitive issues facing our country – and he has drawn on a lifetime of experience. As a member of the Australian Defence Force (ADF), Jim has thought and talked about war for 40 years. He has run a real war as Chief of Operations, primarily for the US forces in Iraq in 2004–05. He has participated in several other operations or activities in our region over those decades, in and with our regional neighbours. And, as a politician and a diplomat, he has been exposed to the complexities of foreign and domestic policy. I have to say, I do not agree with all of Jim's assessments in this book, but even this cursory review of his significant experience and demonstrable capabilities in the defence and national security spheres is enough to show that we should at the very least listen to and debate his arguments.

To deter war, the first step is to understand the problem. Jim makes the argument that due to a reliance on the US for security and prosperity, Australia is lacking resilience in a period of increased strategic competition in our region. I will let Jim defend his assessments, except to say that, in launching the Defence Strategic Update in July 2020, the government outlined how rapidly Australia's strategic environment was deteriorating. It was the recognition of this deterioration and the rapid militarisation of our region that reaffirmed the need for Australia to invest in high-end capabilities that bolster our deterrence and better prepare us to respond in the event of conflict. This in turn led the government to explore the feasibility of acquiring nuclear-powered submarine technology, which culminated with the establishment of AUKUS, the trilateral security pact between Australia, the UK and the US.

In this book, Jim Molan describes his view of the military options that both China and the US would have available should China move to achieve regional dominance. As a military tactician, Jim is aware that it is only through understanding the nature of modern warfare that Australia can prepare correctly to defend its sovereignty and regional stability. Uniquely, Jim links high strategy, concepts of how to fight campaigns, and low-level tactics, all of which must be aligned to be successful in war.

Danger on Our Doorstep reflects on the challenges of international relations within the Indo-Pacific and does so in some detail. A key recent influence on our thinking in this regard has been the Russia–Ukraine War, which has shown that very bad things can happen in this world and that they can happen quickly and with great violence, and that all countries have an obligation to be prepared for them. Jim is able to explain these complex issues in the simplest terms, which is a valuable skill for any politician or author and one recognised by the media, who compete for his valuable commentary, and by the Coalition's base.

Given the sensitive and classified nature of the issues Jim addresses from his unclassified base of knowledge and experience, it will always be difficult for a minister, especially a defence minister, to express an opinion on the merits of a work like *Danger on Our Doorstep*. But I will conclude this foreword by asking, first, is there anyone as credible as Jim to address these issues? And, second, how important is it to appreciate that we live in a country that not only tolerates different views and opinions, but exuberantly defends our right to express them? In that context, this book also represents some of the priceless values we believe are worth fighting for in Australia.

Peter Dutton, April 2022

INTRODUCTION

We had a saying when I was in the military that bad things happen at night, in rain and on the corners of four maps. It refers to a time when wars were fought by commanders looking at maps on paper. In fast-moving operations, you often moved off one map and onto another very quickly, so you needed lots of them. If you found yourself at a corner of one map, it was almost guaranteed that the enemy would have the temerity to be on one of the three adjoining maps, and commanders sometimes had to join maps together with sticky tape, so they ended up about the size of a bedsheet.

I spent a lot of my military life as a light infantryman, often travelling to battles by foot. Everything I needed I carried on my back, so too many maps were a real burden. The only thing worse, though, was not knowing where you were, especially if you had to call for support.

Back in the 'dark ages' – the 1980s – I did an exchange posting to a mechanised British battalion on the NATO front line in northern West Germany. We could see Russian and East German troops across the border and hear them on our radio frequencies. We travelled in tracked armoured personnel carriers, in a total lack of comfort, but our view was that a bad ride was far better than a good walk. As second-in-command of a company of these armoured vehicles, I had hundreds of paper maps. We had to be prepared to move just about anywhere in northern Europe.

Times have changed. The digitisation of just about everything except the rifle and the bayonet has meant that maps can be carried electronically or downloaded to individual commanders when required. Nowadays they are displayed on the equivalent of a mobile-phone-sized personal computer, worn on a soldier's body. All information is captured from space in digital form, then disseminated through the internet or an intranet.

Over 20 years after my time in West Germany, when I was Chief of Operations for the Coalition Forces in Iraq, *all* maps were digitised and displayed on screens. Through sheer habit, I still tended to print certain maps out and jam the paper copy in the 'map pocket' of my pants, just in case the system in my vehicle, known as Blue Force Tracker, failed. Invariably, I would find the paper map unused in my pocket after a day or so, throw it away and replace it with another paper copy.

To produce the maps we worked with in Iraq, every part of the country was put through a process of 'mensuration'. I pretended to know what *mensuration* meant when speaking to smart young US military surveyors, but I took it to mean that every digitised part of the surface of Iraq was fixed by us in space. From my headquarters I could launch a bomb or artillery round or helicopter raid, and everyone involved would know exactly where they were in relation to everyone else. Knowing where everyone is becomes almost the most important thing when you start throwing explosives around.

In Iraq we were lucky. We could move information around our battlefield or between any two points on the surface of the Earth with mind-numbing speed. We had no highly technical enemy opposing us. Our biggest enemy in doing this was normally ourselves. If some lowly staff officer decided that a video of a football match should be seen by all his mates across the operational area, most of our precious bandwidth was consumed. Orders and intelligence would then be distributed by our system so slowly that on several occasions operations had to be delayed or postponed. Each week the US commanding general would announce the 'Bandwidth Pig of the Week' to try and discourage irresponsible use. The hallmark of every headquarters was the large number of satellite dishes, pointing at some satellite in the heavens.

That was 2004 to 2005, a long time ago in terms of data wars. Iraq was, comparatively speaking, a very small and manageable war. The next war will not be like that, because we cannot guarantee our next enemy will be so accommodating. Not only satellites will be used, but also the underground and undersea cables that currently carry our internet, distributed through vast networks of router centres, each the size of a city building. And in the next war they will be one of the first targets of our enemies, as they are the target now of cyber hackers.

We have potential adversaries who are planning and training for exactly these kinds of attacks. In our part of the world, the Indo-Pacific, an aggressive China has the capacity to do this right now. When China talks about the incorporation of the nation of Taiwan into the People's Republic of China by force if necessary, this is shorthand for war. Most of us think this will be a geographically limited war, involving parts of China's coast, the Taiwan Strait and the island of Taiwan itself. If we do ever think about it, we Australians anticipate reading about this war in our newspapers or listening to talking heads on TV. The conflict will take place far from our shores – and life will go on as normal.

But this is not necessarily so. It is more than likely that the first thing we will know about a Taiwan war is that we will not know much about it at all. All our depended-on means of receiving information through the internet and satellites will fail in a single event. And if China decides to act *very* seriously, at the same time as it attacks us in real space and through cyber space, it will use its extraordinary rocket and missile forces to attack US forces in the region. Having done this, China will have pushed the US out and will become the dominant power in the Western Pacific. As for Australia, for the first time since 1942, we will face a region dominated not by our great and powerful friend America, but by a superpower that has since 2016 openly indicated its dislike of us, and twice indirectly threatened us with nuclear attack.

Such a surprise attack has occurred before – at Pearl Harbor in 1941. The US recovered after that but, especially in the early years of World War II, the Allies were also very, very lucky. We will always need luck in wartime but the more we prepare for the right war, the less luck we will need. War with China is possible, and more likely than most leaders are saying, but it is not inevitable. And the more we prepare for the right war, the greater our chance of deterring it, or, in the worst case, minimising its impact. But unless we prepare for the right war, not for the one we would *prefer* to fight, it might be a very good idea to keep a few of those old paper maps handy. In a fight with China, a lot of the electronic devices that drive our plans and our weapons will become as useful as paperweights.

The aim of this book, then, is to answer these questions: what might a regional war with China be like, and how should Australia prepare? Faced with such frightening notions, many Australians will adopt the hope that something as disastrous as this will never happen. They might feel that if it does, Australia should stay aloof. Regional war represents a threat that is recognised by few in the government or bureaucracy, and even less by the Australian people. But given the recent war in Ukraine, which has made state-on-state warfare seem much more possible, and China's increasingly aggressive stance, recognition by Australians of the threat is certainly expanding. After 75 years of relying on the US, Australia has paid for our amazing prosperity by overindulging in globalisation and sacrificing much of our security, and the last thing any of us wants to do is think and talk about war.

I have thought and talked about war for 40 years as a member of the Australian Defence Force (ADF). That was my profession. I have run a real war as Chief of Operations in Iraq and spent years as a soldier in Asia and the South Pacific. I believe I have an intimate knowledge of the US at war and at peace, having trained with the US military at the highest level and fought side by side with the US in Iraq. I also spent five years as a diplomat in Australia's embassy in Indonesia, during the most difficult period of our relationship with that extraordinary country. As I write this, I am a backbench member of the Liberal–National Party Coalition government, which allows me to call myself a partial insider. I have been engaged in the defence and security debate internally with my parliamentary colleagues, and externally, through the media, with the people of Australia.

In this book I aim to tackle themes that are not being addressed elsewhere or widely acknowledged by Australians. Our country may be dangerously weak, but the road to strength does not lie in tackling only one military deficiency after another – submarines, ships, fighters, cyber technology, industrial bases, fuel supplies, military culture – no matter how good the solution to each of these challenges might be. There is danger on our doorstep, and our salvation as a nation lies in aligning high-level strategy with the details of how to fight campaigns (called 'operations' in the military), all the way down to low-level tactics. And the place to start is with what is called a national security strategy, a process of strategic thinking that is used by many of our allies. The first step in such a strategy is to identify the problem, and in national security strategy thinking, the problem is the kind of war that a nation is preparing to fight. Get that wrong and just about everything else is wrong.

My approach here is to describe what some may consider to be a worst-case scenario of war in order to explain how and why I think this 'worst' case is not only possible but likely, and to suggest in this real-politik assessment what Australia's best options are – to avert through deterrence and, if that fails, to respond effectively. This book attempts to answer the question that the Australian government and military refuse even to ask publicly, much less resolve: what war are you preparing for? Only by asking *and* answering this question can Australians decide whether their government is preparing effectively for the right war.

OUT OF THE BLUE?

It's about 10pm on the east coast of Australia when the news services across the nation start to drop off. Within a few minutes, they're gone. Many Australians are already in bed, with few venturing out on this wet, windy night. The year has seen an exceptionally warm and wet summer, but at least COVID-19 and its variants have kept their distance. The last few years have been memorable for all the wrong reasons – drought, fires, floods, plagues, war in Europe, an aggressive superpower in the Western Pacific, even a volcano in the South Pacific, a weak leader in a partisan US, and autocratic leaders across the world becoming more aggressive. At least Australians can comfort themselves that the economy, given the circumstances of world inflation and very high energy prices, has boomed initially after COVID and is still performing quite well, with energy resource prices staying very high. At this hour, in this weather, bed is the only place to be, and as a result very few see the unusual cascade of flashes or 'shooting stars' in the heavens in those places where locally the sky is clear.

Newsroom updates on radio and free-to-air TV include early reports of earthquakes somewhere off the Chinese coast or the nearby Ryukyu Islands, detected by seismographs across the world. The aftershocks are confusing geologists because they show no correlation with previous volcanic activity. Certainly, China's coast is part of the Ring of Fire around the Pacific, so geological activity is to be expected, but still there is no pattern, no consistency, no leadup, just three very loud disturbances. Staff in newsrooms wonder whether a tsunami warning will be issued by the Chinese or Japanese governments; that certainly would be news.

When the emergency generators kick in and the lights come back on, journalists switch on their computers, allow them a few seconds to boot, then enter their IDs and passwords. Nothing happens. This is not a routine outage. The bulletins that can't be broadcast that night won't be issued for several weeks, and by then geological activity will be the least of anyone's concerns. No one, not even in the most secret corridors of government, where backup generators quickly restore the lost connection, can see what the disruptions are, or how far they will go.

At first no one suspects this is an act of war. A few unconnected reports of unusual military and other occurrences on the Chinese mainland have been received by intelligence and media, but most of these are from the previous year. If anything, things in China have quietened down. Those looking for 'the deep, still waters of universal peace',[1] as Australia's Robert Menzies once described them, are even saying that China has been walking back on some of its inflammatory demands. Others think that China might still be absorbing the lessons of the Ukraine War, of which there are many, especially for autocracies. The aggressive form of 'wolf-warrior' diplomacy China practises in its embassies across the world, designed to intimidate its neighbours, has recently been tempered to a mild form of undiplomatic abuse. Australia has even been sent a new ambassador from China, who in his first public speech was more than reasonable and raised the hopes of many for eternal peace and unlimited trade.

The US, like Australia, is fairly relaxed about security, although its surveillance satellites are still constantly monitoring China and Russia (when they are not dodging space junk caused by China and Russia). Nor is the US particularly fazed by reports of civilian Chinese ships taken off routine schedules; of more than the usual number of missile firings on ranges in China's west; of a slight increase in the number of incidents in space, such as the movement of Chinese satellites into orbits that disrupt other satellites; or by an abnormal number of cyber-attacks, probably by a national actor (a country such as China, rather than a criminal group or individuals). These developments can all be explained away.

No one has detected any unusual movements of strategic missiles or nuclear warheads. As far as Western intelligence can tell, there is no worrying number of China's submarines at sea, and China's navy seems to be spending a greater amount of its time in port. North Korea is doing what it always does, blustering and threatening and every now and again firing a test missile into the Sea of Japan. The Russians in Ukraine and a nuclear-armed Iran are considered the biggest current problems for the US.

Artificial intelligence and quantum computing, still in the development stage as predictive tools, have been reporting nothing of great interest, and what has been reported has been discounted as teething problems with these new technologies. Much the same thing had happened with a then brand-new device called 'radar' that was installed on the hills overlooking Pearl Harbor at exactly the time of the Japanese attack in 1941. That new device detected the Japanese attacking aircraft at great range but the warning was rationalised away; the idea of a Japanese attack was beyond comprehension. Just as everyone thought, until Ukraine, that war between great powers, especially in Europe was a thing of the past.

By the time the world's internet starts going down as a result of massive inexplicable failures and unprecedented levels of cyber-attacks, even the surveillance satellites capable of reporting anything have been destroyed by Chinese space-based weapons or other weapons blasted into space from China's mainland and ships at sea. Some of the defence intranets around the world survive, and through these networks it becomes clear that space and internet assets are under purposeful attack; that maybe this is more than just a technical hitch. On the Australian east coast a glance outside military bunkers or media studios shows a sky filled with the 'shooting stars' of satellites burning up. There are lights in the sky, but no light at all in our computer world.

Around the world, control centres watch as the internet tries to revive itself through the automatic rerouting of data. This is supposed to be the strength of the internet, designed as it was to survive a Russian nuclear attack during the Cold War. Yet it still depends for 97% of its traffic not on satellites but on the undersea cables that thread their way through the depths of the world's oceans. Within a few hours, many of these have also gone down, broken by specialist submarines or ships, in addition to space communication and land links. Those cables that remain are considered unreliable; suspicion is high that they have been rerouted, possibly to China, and everything important on them is likely to be read by super computers and foreign analysts.

In national emergency centres and strategic military command centres around the world, the conclusion is very soon reached that some form of major attack has been carried out. But even if this is the case, who has done it, and what can be done in response?

On whatever communication circuits are still operating from London and Brussels to Delhi and Sydney, local officials and military officers are asking questions. Regardless of the answers, action is very limited. In nations where Cold War nuclear attack has been expected in past decades, such as in the UK and the US and in former Eastern Bloc countries, old plans are dusted off and old procedures reinitiated, essentially with everything reverting from centralised to local control. The US nuclear force puts itself on the highest state of alert, but again, no real action can be taken because only the President can initiate the use of nuclear weapons in a counterattack. Only the President has total visibility of the situation – or that is how it is supposed to happen. In this case, when every action so far detected cannot be confidently attributed to a particular country, who should the President defend against or attack?

As communication systems across the world progressively go down, the US national command system with the President at the top is not even aware that, by midnight, Chinese missiles are being readied for launch in their fortified hiding places across China, to be fired at a selection of targets throughout the Western Pacific and elsewhere, such as Diego Garcia, a US military base in the Indian Ocean, and possibly even Australia. These missiles are not detected at launch because most of the assets that would normally do so, such as early-warning satellites, have been rendered inoperable or, if they are still working, cannot communicate with their controllers. The launch of the missiles against disparate targets has been coordinated by China so that they impact almost simultaneously on the US air force and naval bases in the Western Pacific, including armouries in those locations holding US nuclear weapons, and on Diego Garcia.

The Chinese missiles are carrying only high-explosive warheads, not nuclear ones. But they have an accuracy of 5 to 10 metres through mid-course correction and do not require a large number of hits on each base to be effective. Ten or so missiles targeted at key points at each base are enough to render these critical facilities inoperable for a long time into the future, and to destroy aircraft and ships there at the time of the strike. Just as in 1941 in Pearl Harbor, US aircraft, including fighters, tankers, surveillance aircraft, bombers and intelligence-collecting aircraft, are mostly parked in neat straight lines clearly visible from space. The Chinese targeteers – the military operatives who coordinate complex attacks – do not make the same mistake as the Japanese when they attacked Pearl Harbor, by failing to destroy the fuel storage tanks which later refuelled the replacement aircraft carriers that ultimately defeated the Japanese Imperial Navy.

With no expectation of an immediate attack the US bases have been operating to a peacetime routine. Their commanders have been screaming for years about how vulnerable they are to such an attack, but Congress and the President denied them the funds to build an adequate number of shelters to protect the aircraft, to ring their airfields, ports and facilities such as armouries or fuel storage tanks with defensive missiles, or to disperse their aircraft to other locations – in other words, to 'harden' their bases. What good is an aircraft carrier without aircraft? What good are fighter or bomber aircraft on local bases without tanker aircraft? What good is shipping in replacement cargoes of fuel, spare parts and weapons if there are no port facilities? What good are air refuelling tankers without the fuel to fill them? And finally, the biggest question of all, what good is US military power in the Western Pacific without the bases from which to project that power?

Once hit, the 'flight lines', as the aircraft parking spaces are called, burn for days and make reinforcement of the Western Pacific by the US from its worldwide forces almost impossible, or at least immensely complex, slow and vulnerable. Just to make sure that any essential targets do not survive, a second wave of cruise missiles is fired from ships, submarines and large bombers. These missiles are soon winging their way at just below the speed of sound and just above the surface of the sea towards what is left of the US bases. Their job is to prevent any chance that the bases can be brought back to a functioning state. As the waves of missiles approach their targets at sea level, they climb suddenly so that their radars and optical systems can look down and lock onto their targets for the final few seconds of their flight. In most cases they smash into burning piles of wreckage, but their psychological effect, where there is enough daylight to see them as they rise in waves and then attack with merciless accuracy, is as significant as the physical damage.

In or near bases, local commanders, staff and emergency services are completely consumed for the next few days with handling casualties, re-establishing basic communications back to Hawaii or Washington, and considering what they might be able to do next. What can they do? They have no aviation fuel to pour into any new refuelling tankers that might be flown in from somewhere else, such as the US or Europe. The massive amount of fuel that these bases consume can be supplied by local civilian refineries but only for a short period of time, and only if the piping and the storage is at least partly working. Most bases depend on shipping to bring in bulk supplies of petroleum products, and that will take weeks or months, not days.

Nor do the bases have repair facilities now for the military equipment they support. Modern aircraft demand a high level of maintenance by very skilled maintainers with a guaranteed supply of spare parts, and ships are even more demanding. Even if the destroyed attack aircraft (also known as fighters) can be replaced from other parts of the world, they will need their own maintenance crews and spare parts, which will have to be flown in by transport aircraft before the attack aircraft arrive. And nothing at that scale and across the mighty Pacific can happen fast.

Moreover, the bases' stocks of bombs and missiles have all been destroyed, so even if by superhuman effort they were able to obtain the fuel, the aircraft and the maintenance staff, they have no armaments. And unless the US can establish anti-aircraft and anti-missile units around the bases to defend against the kind of missile attacks they have just suffered, the Chinese can simply re-attack the bases when they see them approaching a revived operational state.

* * *

The US has 11 nuclear-powered attack submarines active in the Pacific at the time of the devastating attack. A few of these are in the vicinity of Taiwan, and several others are tracking Chinese ballistic missile submarines (known as 'boomers') in the East and South China seas. The 'boomers' have not tried to launch nuclear missiles, so no action is *taken against them by the trailing US submarines. One of the US submarines in the navy fleet, armed with a large number of missiles originally designed to attack targets on land but now also capable of attacking ships, is on patrol near Taiwan and monitors strange rumblings in its vicinity. The listening devices on board this submarine are so sensitive they can detect whales talking to each other oceans away, so, unlike the geologists, the crew know that the noises they hear are not volcanoes or earthquakes because, when the initial explosive noises die away, the submariners can hear the sounds of other ships or submarines breaking up under water. But even though the crew have an idea of what is happening, there is no quick way to report it; the sophisticated comms systems, which depend on space communications, very low frequency radio waves and then various cyber systems, are so degraded as to be inoperative.*

What the US crew know from what they can hear is that China has probably detonated nuclear depth charges under water (the one exception to China's self-imposed non-nuclear rule) and that the other three US subs may have been destroyed. The detonations occurred a little while before the main attack on the US bases and were coordinated as much as possible with the attacks on space satellites and cyber-attacks on the internet. While China knew roughly where the US submarines in the vicinity of Taiwan were, they did not know precisely. The massive blast power of the nuclear depth charges meant any submarine in the wider area would be destroyed.

These nuclear depth charges are a killer weapon that the US, the UK and the Russians developed to use against each other during the Cold War. The US and the UK apparently stopped their development – at least unclassified sources said so. The Chinese secretly took up the idea, and by this stage have a number of working models deployed either by ship or aircraft or linked to seabed sensor arrays that listen to all the noises of the ocean and can detect even the quietest submarines.

The US Pacific Fleet has only two groupings of ships deployed in the region at the time of the attack, which is fairly normal for the past few years. The first is a carrier strike group based around the USS Gerald R. Ford, which consists of seven warships and one submarine plus a logistic support ship. This group entered the South China Sea through Luzon Strait in the Philippines, intending to split up and make visits to various ports in the Philippines to celebrate the re-establishment of the defence pact between that nation and the US. It then planned to exit the South China Sea and head back to more distant waters – not because it might be under greater threat from China than normal, but because the US government did not want to annoy China while ongoing negotiations on climate agreements were in progress.

The second group consists of seven ships carrying a US Marine Corps unit of several thousand soldiers, all their vehicles, aircraft and equipment – known as the expeditionary strike group. After six months away on a deployment in the Persian Gulf, living on board their ships as marines do, they are transiting back to their Japanese home base and, after a brief stop in Perth, are threading their way through the Indonesian Archipelago. Like the carrier strike group, the expeditionary strike group is proceeding in a peaceful manner, unaware that its location is being intensely monitored by China's satellites and that its fate is sealed.

All the ballistic and cruise missiles that China launches on this night to attack the US ships have maximum ranges of between 1000 and 5000 kilometres. They can reach out into the Pacific as far as Guam (approximately 4000 kilometres away) in the south-west, and as far south as parts of Papua New Guinea (approximately 5000 kilometres away). They include a missile referred to as the 'carrier killer', which the Chinese claim can hit and destroy a US aircraft carrier – a particularly difficult target as it moves and manoeuvres on the ocean. All the missiles attacking the ships in these two battle groups are conventionally armed with non-nuclear warheads and up to a tonne of high explosives.

The missiles launch against the ships just as the US command system across the world loses communications.

Carrier-killer missiles from China's east and south coasts are fired at the larger ships in both battle groups, with backup from smaller cruise missiles from Chinese ships and submarines in the vicinity, and from China's old but usable H-6 bombers, which each fire two of the enormous anti-ship cruise missiles they haul into the air under their wings.

The conflagration among these two battle groups is reminiscent of naval battles in the Pacific during World War II. There are no mushroom clouds, but crimson explosions bloom as the missiles penetrate the flight decks of the carriers, fuel is ignited and weapons magazines explode, tearing these gigantic ships and their thousands of crew members to bits. Several of the accompanying cruisers are also hit and break apart. The wrecks burn red until they sink, as smaller supporting ships move in to try and rescue troops or train hoses on the fires. But these ships too are soon hit by missiles and lost. The cost in human lives is appalling.

The aim of the Chinese is not to destroy every ship in the two groups, or even a large number of ships in the Pacific Fleet, because they know that the US can bring more ships into the Pacific. But they have sent a clear message: we are the dominant power in the region. We can destroy the US Navy.

* * *

It is not just an attack on US forces that occurs on this disastrous night, however. Strikes are also launched against US allies Japan, South Korea and Australia. China's attacks on US bases in Japan kill tens of thousands of Americans and many thousands of Japanese on the bases or in their vicinity. China does not attack Japan's military forces, which are not insignificant and of high quality, reasoning that its own missile stocks are not infinite and that some have to be held in reserve, and that the US will be so hurt in the Western Pacific by the initial attacks that Japan will not fight on while the bases are burning and the Japanese first responders are still digging out their casualties. It is a critical assumption that remains to be tested. But even if Japan does not accept the inevitable – Chinese dominance of the region – China still has the ability and the opportunity to use force later if it is needed.

South Korea, another key US ally, is not considered by China to be a force that needs to be dealt with at this stage, because north across the border there are one million North Korean troops who represent the most imminent threat to that country. Both Japan and South Korea will be docile, China reckons, if the US forces in the Western Pacific are destroyed.

Australia is a slightly different matter. The Chinese hope – indeed expect – that the US will now acknowledge China as paramount in the Western Pacific. This is the most *logical course of action from China's point of view. The US can withdraw all the way to its hemisphere and redefine its sphere of influence as east of Hawaii. The American people, China reasons and hopes, will not be prepared to shoulder the burden of world leadership as they did during World War II, and pay the price of hundreds of thousands of dead.*

Yet China cannot blindly rely on this hope. It has to consider the possibility that the US might fight back, and the most likely way to do this (without using nuclear weapons) is by assembling both its allies and its military forces from around the world. Trade sanctions and other US-initiated actions in the UN will of course occur, but the US will have to prepare itself for offensive action sometime in the future or surrender world power to China. Mobilising military forces and shifting them to the Pacific from the US and from Europe will take time and will need a firm base, a trusted ally somewhere in the region closer than Hawaii. Australia is likely to be that base, China has reasoned, and it will therefore have to be dealt with in this first round of attacks.

To this end, eight Chinese submarines have been deployed to four critical locations around the Australian continent. Cruise missiles launched from the subs are easily able to destroy Australia's fleet of F-18F Super Hornet fighters, Growler electronic warfare aircraft and most of the F-35 fighter aircraft sitting on criminally unprotected bases in the north and the east of the country. The attack is of a different scale from that prosecuted against US bases, but it is as effective against Australia's small but very technologically advanced air force as the larger missiles are against US bases. As Australians try to work out what is going on in a world deprived of its normal means of communications, and as its defence forces try to switch to backup systems that are slow and intermittent, the government receives information that Australia is under attack as well, and its small but beautiful air force has been destroyed.

Over the next day or so, the Chinese submarines silently move to new attack positions. Lurking just off the coast, they dispatch automated and self-propelled sea mines to the vicinity of key military facilities in the harbours of Darwin, Sydney and Garden Island south of Perth. These advanced, unmanned undersea weapons, with sensors able to identify any type of ship passing by, travel to a predetermined position and stay there. They are programmed to destroy any warships that attempt to move out of the harbours, effectively locking them in. No one has any idea how many of these sophisticated mines have been deployed and it takes some time to sweep the harbours clear of them, and free the Australian fleets.

Joint US and Australian communication facilities in Australia remain physically untouched; the Chinese logic is that so many other parts of the US early-warning and submarine-communications system have been destroyed that it is not worth wasting longer-range missiles or cruise missiles from submarines on other targets, especially those far inland on the Australian continent, such as the sites of the over-the-horizon early-warning radar collectively known as Jindalee.

China has taken a step from which there is no retreat. It knows that after its space and cyber-attacks, after striking US bases in the region, destroying two US battle groups and several nuclear submarines, but particularly with the killing of a large number of Americans, it has redefined the power struggle in the Western Pacific and perhaps across the world.

CHAPTER 1

RISE TO POWER

It is my belief that a war with China – perhaps resembling the scenario outlined in the previous pages – is possible, and that it is more likely than most Australian commentators, and indeed most world leaders, are saying. These are not just my views but the views of US and other military commanders and regional defence ministers.[1] And a growing number of Australian politicians subscribe to these views too.

War is not inevitable, but whether it occurs or not is likely to depend on the strength and resolve of the US and its allies, including Australia. This question of likelihood must not be dismissed by the false hope that war is so appalling that it could never occur, or the probability is small enough to be ignored. We need a strategy based on the real world, and not on how we *hope* the world is.

China and other regional powers are armed and are talking tough, and many have competing interests.[2] But why is China most likely to be our foe, how has it attained a level of military power capable of threatening the global balance of power, and what would it be seeking to achieve by triggering a regional conflict?

Like Germany and Japan before it, the military power of the People's Republic of China (PRC) has increased exponentially under its more modern authoritarian leaders,[3] and China is now searching for spheres of influence in Asia and beyond and trying to control critical technologies and resources. It is not only the leaders who have created this militarisation of the state but many causes working together: strong centralised leadership by presidents and the

Chinese soldiers on parade in the Forbidden City in Beijing. China has the world's largest army, navy, militia, non-nuclear rocket force and homeland air defence. *(Getty)*

Chinese Communist Party (CCP); strong memories of recent experiences of aggression towards China, which reduced it to an effective colony for over 100 years; an ideology around the CCP that put the party and common good before the rights of the individual; technology and industry, some of it stolen from its competitors, that is as good as anything in the world; the ability to control populations through technology rather than through coercion; and the willingness of the people to accept that the military and the civilian spheres of their lives are one. Prussian militarism and Japanese imperialism had nothing on the militarisation of China under the CCP, especially in the years since Xi Jinping became president in 2013.

China under the CCP claims special legitimacy as a many-thousand-year-old nation with exceptional culture and traditions, and regards the PRC as merely an extension of ancient China. BBC journalist Bill Hayton in his 2020 book *The Invention of China* addresses these points, and characterises the political ideology of the CCP as 'national-socialism with Chinese characteristics'.[4] How else, he asks, to describe a system featuring a 'core leader, insistent demands for natural homogeneity, intolerance of difference, rule by party not by law, corporativist economic policies, a focus on discipline and an ideology based on tactical exceptionalism – all backed up by a massive surveillance state'?[5] Others have continued the Nazi Germany analogy.

Journalist Daryl McCann notes in a review of Hayton's work, that 'the unbridled ambitions of Xi Jinping's foreign policy reverberate with the hubris of the Third Reich in the lead up to the second world war'.[6]

Like Nazi Germany, communist China is a modern construction, not a unique 5000-year-old civilisation, although Han chauvinism is certainly not identical with Nazi Aryanism. 'Exterminationist antisemitism' (a hatred of Jews involving extermination of the race) does not lie at the heart of President Xi Jinping's so-called Chinese Dream. That said, notions of racial superiority are key to the CCP's *modus operandi*.[7] Just ask the Uighurs, and the Tibetans, both peoples whose rights have been severely impinged.

China is a revisionist nation that sees its place in the family of nations as the dominant power at least in this region, and ultimately in the world. China does not accept the status quo that has made it rich and powerful, a status quo built on the security provided to the world economy and to its trade routes by US power and influence, including military power. China has demonstrated that it has no respect for international law and conventions through its claims in the South China Sea, the militarisation of islands and reefs contrary to international law, and its treatment of its populations in its Muslim areas, in Tibet and in Hong Kong.[8] Being dominant is strongly related to the continuance in power of the CCP. And this is a zero-sum game for China. China must reduce US power and influence to increase its own.

Modern China is a highly sophisticated, technologically advanced, militarised, industrialised nation of 1.3 billion people, with the biggest sense of insecurity in the world. Part of this insecurity is based on the appalling abuse inflicted on China not only by the West, especially the British during the Opium Wars, but also by Japan during its murderous invasion before and during World War II. The years between the unravelling of the Qing Dynasty, beginning in 1839, and the ascent of the CCP are known as China's 100 years of national humiliation. This sense of insecurity, shared by the Chinese people as a whole, is reinforced regularly by CCP propaganda. China will never forget or forgive.

China's technological and industrial base has produced a military machine of daunting capability, supported by civilian efforts. The West won the Cold War against the Soviet Union because its industrial and technological base was far greater. But China has been so successful in modern industrialisation that the difference between soldier, scientist, technologist and civilian is hardly perceptible. China's national aim is to ensure it is never in such a position of weakness that it can be so humiliated again. And this seems reasonable to most Chinese.

Of course, the party still has to consider the mood of the people, and it has done this fastidiously. The State has given the people as much prosperity as it can afford, while, with few exceptions, its citizens have gratefully and proudly accepted this prosperity at the cost of certain individual liberties. They have done this because they, their parents or their grandparents remember how much suffering the Chinese people endured in earlier times, or because, as with most younger people, they have been constantly told of this suffering by the party. Like good people everywhere, the Chinese just want to live in peace, enjoy life, educate their children and increase their prosperity. The price for doing this, they believe, is to faithfully support the CCP.

Although today's nation of China – as reinvented by the party – is as modern a creation as any other nation in the world, the Chinese people believe in the nation's myths and legends. Perhaps the most enduring of those myths is that the island of Taiwan is rightfully part of China. The CCP has staked part of its legitimacy on the question of 'reincorporating' Taiwan into the PRC and has been saying for decades that Taiwan will be returned to China, even if force must be used.

For thousands of years, Taiwan was a home to local tribes and was seen as a source of natural resources including gold and sulphur, which were mined by Chinese interests and, in more modern times, various colonising powers. In 1662, after the Manchus overthrew the Ming Dynasty on the Chinese mainland, the Ming loyalists retreated to

Taiwan and threw out the foreign miners, mainly Dutch, but were themselves defeated 20 years later by the Manchu Qing Dynasty. In 1885, the Qing empire designated Taiwan as China's twenty-second province. In the First Sino-Japanese War of 1894–95, China was defeated by Japan and ceded Taiwan, which the Japanese then occupied until 1945.

After Japan's defeat in World War II, the island was taken over by the Chinese Nationalist Party and returned to China's control. But after the Chinese Communists defeated the Nationalists in the Chinese Civil War, in 1948, the Nationalists retreated to Taiwan and established the island as a base for their plan to reconquer the Chinese mainland. The PRC, led by Mao Zedong, was determined to liberate Taiwan from the Nationalists but was unable to do so mainly because of the presence of US forces in the region, especially US naval forces in the Taiwan Strait. Taiwan, which was never part of the PRC, has been an independent country since that time – much to the chagrin of China.

Another strongly held belief, and one of the most contentious international issues for China, is that it should control the South China Sea. This stretch of water, along with the East China Sea, is considered to be of crucial importance to the country's strategic security. Since the late 1940s, China has claimed all of the South China Sea as its sovereign territory. It bases its claim on maps produced by the Chinese themselves in the 1920s and 1940s, one of which showed a nine-dash line running from Taiwan south along the coast of the Philippines, swinging west past the island of Borneo, then turning north past the Vietnam coast to Hainan.

The nine-dash line encompasses many island groups claimed by other nations, including the Spratly Islands and the Paracel Islands. Using the line to justify its actions, China has in recent decades constructed military facilities, including harbours and airstrips, on some of these islands. The validity of China's claim over this maritime area was legally tested in 2016, when the Permanent Court of Arbitration in The Hague ruled that China had no claim. China strongly rejected that determination and continues to use the nine-dash line to validate its ongoing attempts to control these territories and support its view that what the rest of the world calls international law is irrelevant.

CHAPTER 2

PLAYING CATCH-UP

Until the twenty-first century, China had limited military tools that it could use to achieve its geopolitical goals. But recently it has made astonishingly rapid progress in developing and expanding its military, and it now has vastly greater firepower and far more strategic options at its disposal.

Tracking this development in a secretive and strongly authoritarian country like China from outside is no easy task. To assess progress, it's essential to constantly monitor press reports and official statements and deduce from these and the appearance of new rocket systems, nuclear submarines, stealth technology and the like when such programs might have started, how they progressed, who ran them and so on. I've been doing this for the last three decades and the following account is based on that long experience.

China's level of technology in the late twentieth century meant it could control the air and sea approaches to China and Taiwan only to the limits of its ability. That in turn meant that if it wanted to retake Taiwan it would have to send its forces by air and sea across the Taiwan Strait to disembark on the island's shores, in a similar way to the D-Day landing of 1944, then secure the island and wait for the US and the rest of the world to react.

Military leaders assumed that the US response would come initially from nuclear submarines in the vicinity of Taiwan sending up flights of conventional (non-nuclear) missiles from below the surface, as far as 1000 kilometres away from their targets, or from long-range torpedoes fired from the vicinity of the Taiwan Strait. China's analysis showed that this might cost China up to one-third of its invasion force over a couple of days. And for some time, as China put together a military that had the capacity to invade Taiwan, it was prepared to accept this loss; there was no other choice. It also accepted the losses that would come to such an invasion force when US air bases in Japan, South Korea, Guam, Diego Garcia, Alaska and Hawaii, or even further away, mounted the expected retaliatory strikes on Chinese bases and air and sea invasion fleets.

However, through the 1990s and early 2000s, as China's mastery of space, cyber, missile and rocket technology enhanced the warfighting capacity of all branches of the People's Liberation Army, as Russia's willingness to provide weapons that China could copy increased, and as US power did not expand in line with China's, broader military options in relation to Taiwan came to be considered. Furthermore, as China's industry, technology, infrastructure and military expanded, and its cashed-up businessmen and entrepreneurs spread throughout the world, buying and trading and giving ballast to the emerging superpower and to its military, so did the country's confidence rise.

Yet even as its military capabilities grew, there were still some assumptions to which China remained committed. The first was to avoid war if possible, but to prepare every part of the nation, not just the military, for war if it became necessary. The second was that if force were to be used, it would not involve nuclear weapons, again unless absolutely necessary. A third consideration, however, was that if China was to be dominant, at least initially in the Western Pacific, the US would have to be dealt with there. The fourth was that war, if required to deal with the US and regain Taiwan, was likely to cause the largest geopolitical upheaval in a century. The biggest question for the Chinese leadership in considering contingency plans for a regional war was how to incorporate these four theoretical considerations within a practical plan for military action.

Over the course of decades, the Chinese had reasoned that the best way to ensure any war would stay non-nuclear was to strengthen its own nuclear rocket force as a deterrent. This was gradually achieved. It took the US intelligence services several years to determine that China's nuclear warhead tally had passed 400, something they announced only in 2021. In all probability, China by then could have been at 1000 warheads, a figure that the Western media had previously predicted China would not attain until 2030.

Chinese military leaders studied the war methods used by the US in the Persian Gulf during 1990 and 1991 and reached some very important conclusions. The first was to acknowledge the decisive US victory over Iraq's forces, who relied on Russian weapons and tactics, as did China at that time. The US achieved its victory using its own Cold War-era weapons and tactics, which were far superior to anything China possessed. China also noted how long the US took to build up its military strength in the region – about six months – and that, when it did finally act, its victory was almost total. It stalled only because the US did not want to risking losing its allies, and because US leadership objected morally to the final destruction of the Iraqi armed forces as they streamed helplessly out of Kuwait.

China concluded it could imitate and improve on US tactics when the time came for its own attacks. It admired the coordination of military action that the US almost took for granted, and also saw how dependent the US was on the so-called revolution in military affairs – that is, the harnessing of civilian information technology for military use. China realised it could learn these operational techniques, or it could fight in a way that would render such techniques less important, especially in a war with the US in China's backyard. The US had achieved great things in its reliance initially on technology and industry and more recently on cyber and space technology, and the Chinese would have to do the same to exploit US vulnerabilities.

In terms of military hardware, initially China concluded that it could not compete with American aircraft technology as demonstrated in the Gulf, at least not for a decade or so, but that it *could* compete in the areas of missiles and rocketry. So China focused on these areas, producing a world-leading rocket and missile force. Soon after the year 2000, China turned its attention back to its air force and began to develop aircraft that were competitive with US combat aircraft, especially in relation to the reliability of engines, computing technology and invisibility to radar (known as 'stealth'), often based on information technology stolen from the US and Europe.

Following its success in developing and modernising its industrial base, infrastructure and human capital, China soon had much more to protect than in revolutionary times. It had long been confident that its massive tunnel systems would safeguard its military assets until they were deployed for action. Now it also hardened its east-coast military bases, making them as impervious as possible to missile, rocket or bomb attack, and enabling them to recover quickly if such an attack took place. Its submarines were safe in their pens and could enter and leave their base on the island of Hainan under water. There even arose a belief that, because of the size of its population and its preparations, China was the only nation on Earth that could sustain a nuclear attack and, as a nation, survive.

The only real vulnerability that China had in this period when its military power was still somewhat limited was its surface fleet, which could not be shielded and would have to be deployed and manoeuvre to protect itself. So the country developed an air-defence system, based on short- and long-range missile systems initially procured from Russia, which it copied then manufactured locally. These missiles could cover some of the most important parts of China and its eastern cities, while mobile units could dominate Taiwan and its approaches from as far away as the Chinese mainland. In the event of an attack on Taiwan, this would at least weaken the impact of US air power and provide some protection for China's fleets when they were in their ports or even while transiting the Taiwan Strait.

As China steadily increased its firepower, its military planners must have been astonished that the US increasingly dismissed China as a potential threat and dedicated almost all its research and development and military innovation to counter-terrorism and counter-insurgency, rather than pouring money into the rocketry, fighters, naval self-defence, strike-hardened regional bases and large military forces that were necessary to maintain its advantage in the Pacific sphere. The real deficiencies for the US in the post-Reagan era started with the Gulf War of 1990 and carried through the Afghanistan War of 2001 and the Iraq War of 2003, which wore out both national resolve and military equipment at great national cost. The development of key future technologies was delayed in order to fight 'today's wars' in Iraq and Afghanistan. The decline of US military capacity continued under President Obama, who reduced the defence budget severely, and it was not helped by President Trump, who talked a strong game but never quite got around to spending effectively on defence. There is no sign of a Reagan-like president in the wings, who is willing to focus the US on what is really important.

All through this period the US military was aware of its weaknesses, revealed in wargame after wargame. A few generals broke their silence, and a few politicians tried to get Congress to focus, while the US military attempted to do even more with even less. In its inimitable manner, the military did its best to solve the problems essentially created by US civilian leadership. It re-examined the way it might fight a war with China with inadequate forces by making changes to its operational concepts – that is, *how* it fights. But clever concepts and tactics need to be based on even smarter strategy, and that has been missing in the US, and in many allied countries, in recent times.

One thing that Chinese military strategists could see as they studied their adversary towards the end of its involvement in Iraq and Afghanistan was that the US just did not have enough attack aircraft. The limited range of most US aircraft, almost all of which were older than the best Chinese aircraft and designed for short-range wars in Europe, negated the ability of the few US stealth planes that could avoid radar detection. Even if a small number of US stealth aircraft could get through the Chinese missile screen, bomb a target and get out, the most important Chinese targets were now either impervious to such attacks because they had been hardened, required repeated attacks to breach, or were strongly defended by missiles. Such a situation meant that the risks that China faced in achieving its aims in the Western Pacific were becoming less daunting.

China's military leadership also recognised that Pacific geography and the long distances US aircraft had to travel from regional bases to targets made them totally dependent on aerial refuelling. The US air refuelling fleet had expanded as a result of the need to prepare for a potential war in Europe or South Korea and was truly enormous, consisting of over 700 adapted civilian airliners. In an air battle close to China's shores, these lumbering tanker aircraft would sit in a line a few hundred kilometres from the targets of

If China were able to destroy US air tankers during a conflict in the Western Pacific, US fighters would soon run out of fuel and plummet into the ocean. *(Getty)*

the US attack formations in order to refuel aircraft going into China and then coming back out. China realised that the refuelling tankers were a weakness and that it had the missile technology to attack them. China's regiments of older fighters could transport the latest long-range missiles to launch points and fire them as the tankers flew lazy circles in the sky, waiting for returning fighters and bombers.

So Chinese wargames concentrated on this vulnerable tanker line, rather than on the stealthy attack aircraft. Even the stealthiest of US aircraft needed refuelling to get back to base after an attack, and if many or all of the tankers had already been hit by China's air-to-air missiles, these superb US fighter aircraft, designed for shorter-range wars against

Russia in Europe, would splash harmlessly into the ocean after they ran out of fuel. There would be few follow-up attacks, and the US stealth technology – which China soon gained after stealing it from the Americans – would rot at the bottom of the sea.

The Chinese were aware that if they invaded Taiwan they would be subject to attack by aircraft from US aircraft carriers. It's publicly known that only one US carrier attack group, with its 'air wing' of 70 aircraft, is likely to be in the Pacific at any one time during routine peacetime deployments. But if the US is given warning, it can deploy up to three aircraft carriers relatively quickly and, over time, even more. Chinese forces therefore needed to be strong enough to deal with at least one carrier strike group immediately, and maybe one or two more in the short to medium term. As Chinese missile and rocket technology became more and more sophisticated, this goal appeared attainable.

Carrier strike groups suffer from the limits imposed by Pacific geography on all forces. China gradually built up enough accurate missiles to destroy most of these ships – as long as it could defend its space-based targeting system. It does not matter how accurate a missile is if the location of its target is either not known, or the target, possibly an aircraft carrier underway on the high seas, moves after the missile is launched. The initial location of a target would be detected by surveillance satellites, or by very sophisticated long-range land-based radars located in China itself, and this data then passed to the launch sites. Such targeting data is sufficient for the missile to be fired, but if the target is moving, the aim point of the missile has to be continually adjusted while the missile is in flight. This is technologically very difficult to do, and because it depends so much on space systems, any such technique is vulnerable to weapons that might be used against it in space.

If US aircraft carriers moved to points from where they could launch attacks by air against mainland targets, they would be well within the range of China's missiles. In surface-fleet action, the advantage goes to whoever fires first, and who has the longer-range weapons. And the key advantage in missile range has been moving in China's favour for some years.

For some time, the greatest dangers to the US surface fleet have been two types of Chinese missile that have gained fearsome reputations around the world. The DF-21D 'carrier killer' carries up to a tonne of conventional explosive, and has an accuracy of 20 metres over thousands of kilometres, even if the target is moving. It can be fired above the Earth's atmosphere from the Chinese mainland and travel at many times the speed of sound, and its flight path can be corrected mid-course. By the time a fleet-on-fleet engagement is possible, US ships within range will have been attacked decisively. The second kind of missile, the DF-26, or 'Guam killer', is the largest air-launched cruise missile in the world and is carried by a Chinese aircraft to its launch point, from where it 'cruises' to its target, staying within the atmosphere. The US Navy, the greatest navy in the world, is now vulnerable if it chooses to fight within range of these missiles – if the US wants to become involved in a Chinese invasion of Taiwan.

China's military planners have also grown increasingly confident that they have the technology to attack US surveillance and communication systems in space, at least during critical periods. At the same time, their massive cyber capability can be focused on preventing the US and its allies from conveying critical warfighting data around the world. Even if some US or allied systems in space survive a Chinese attack, once China gains control of ground links through cyber-attacks or other actions, the surveillance systems will be rendered incapable of conveying what they see or hear to terrestrial command centres. China also has the ability to secretly redirect the seabed communication cables that carry most of the world's supposedly secure internet data to monitoring centres that study and collect useful information. In addition, China has planned for specially designed submarines to simply cut the cables at vulnerable points. The advantage that the US has enjoyed for many years through its advanced technology and industry no longer exists.

The last challenge for China's military planners with regard to potential wars in the Western Pacific was to align *how* it would fight – its 'operations' – with the tactical capability of the specific weapons and techniques that progress had delivered. Once that was resolved, the generals could confidently offer China's political leadership war plans to achieve their national strategic objectives. No longer did China have to accept that it would have to absorb US attacks on its mainland bases and its deployed invasion forces during a D-Day-style invasion of Taiwan. Instead, it could link two of the most potent techniques of war – deception and surprise – using its missiles and other weapons, giving it the ability to spring a devastating attack on US regional bases that would remove US power from the Western Pacific and leave China free to resolve the Taiwan issue in its own time, without any interference.

Even after these goals were achieved, Chinese generals were unlikely to make a case for war to the president; that's not the culture of this authoritarian nation. But it might be different if a near-deified leader asked, 'Why attack Taiwan first and then wait for the US, the region and the world to react? Why not attack US bases, which we know to be vulnerable, as well as the US fleet if it approaches? And only once US bases are put out of action and the US fleet is damaged, if not destroyed, *then* attack Taiwan?'

If they were given the opening they were secretly hoping for, the generals would begin coordinating their complex plans. One of their first objectives would be to create the kind of national resilience that China would need if it were to fight a war. That would require China to build up at least a year's reserves of strategic materials, including microchips, or to establish alternative sources of supply that could be trusted.

For commercial reasons, China has already commenced this process, amassing natural resources such as coal, oil and iron ore. It has opened up rail lines into Russia and is shipping iron ore and coal across the Amur River border to reduce its dependence on resources from US allies like Australia. And instead of being imported via vulnerable shipping routes through international waters or US-controlled territories, oil from the Middle East and from the Central Asian nations known as the 'Stans' is now flowing through pipelines, straight into China.

CHAPTER 3

WOLF WARRIORS

No other country in world history has moved up the power ladder as fast as China has over the last decade or so. From coming into being in 1948 at the bottom of the ladder as a primarily agrarian nation and economy with next to no industry, China has lifted the majority of its people out of poverty and has created a sustainable economic society with a level of industry and technology that is the envy of the world. It is far from perfect but stands in contrast to so many countries in Asia and Africa that have started from a higher base yet have not reached the heights of China's achievements. Today China can comfortably sustain a military that is regionally dominant. And now, disturbingly, this extraordinary nation is becoming irrationally aggressive.[1]

When President Xi arrived on the scene as paramount leader in 2013, China was already melding its civilian and military worlds into one. As a powerful dictator in an authoritarian system, Xi could ensure that if the Chinese state wanted something to happen, it would happen with the greatest of rapidity. And while for much of its history the CCP had relied on fear and coercion to achieve its authoritarian aims, now it could place greater emphasis on incentives such as access to a prosperous life for a large number of people. The China Xi has created is far different from that of the nation headed by the pragmatic Deng Xiaoping, who opened China up to the outside world, and promoted modernisation of the economy and what was essentially a form of capitalism – 'socialism with Chinese characteristics', as it was known.

Xi has made a profound difference to China by enacting an aggressive foreign policy, supported by so-called wolf-warrior diplomacy, the effects of which have been seen already in China–Japan relations, in Africa and in Eurasia, and in the trade sanctions that were applied to Australia after its leaders supported an inquiry into the source of the COVID-19 pandemic.

We saw Germany wage war in 1914 to prevent its hegemonic aspirations from being crushed by a British–Russian–French entente, and Australia was drawn into that conflict at the cost of over 50,000 killed, even though we were from the far side of the world. In 1941, in our neighbourhood, Japan waged war to prevent the US from choking its empire, and this war was a direct threat to Australia. Japan conducted what was supposed to be a lightning war to gain access to Dutch East Indies' oil, which it did successfully. Japan then tried to establish an economic bloc in the area of its conquered states known as the Greater East Asia Co-prosperity Sphere, which at that time included most of Manchuria and China.

In recent times, China has been acting in ways that are frighteningly similar to Germany and Japan in those two world conflicts. In both those cases, either individual leaders and/or their parties provided decisive leadership that led to a national desire for empire. In China's case, the appearance of President Xi as the paramount leader was decisive. Under Xi, China has claimed the South China Sea as its own, citing dubious historical justification; encouraged the advance of Chinese interests into Africa and other parts of Asia and the Pacific; increased social control of ethnic minorities such as the Uighurs in Xinjiang region; and clamped down on democratic movements in Hong Kong. Furthermore, since 2014, gambling on the weakness of any US-led opposition, China has engaged in a truly massive nationwide construction effort in the South China Sea, building islands that it has then duplicitously fortified, militarising the area and pushing China's controlled territory another 1000 kilometres out from its coast. Not only has this improved China's coastal defences, but it also means China can control all civil shipping through this area when it wants to. And it has started to apply strictures to international shipping already, demanding a reporting system and more information on individual ships than it has any right to collect.

China keeps testing the waters to see how much can be gained short of the massive use of armed force. As well as its total control of Hong Kong against every assurance given and its illegal militarisation of islands in the South China Sea, examples of it trying to have its own way include its bullying and its sanctioning of trade restrictions on other countries, as well as its actions on the Indian border. China has also opposed a Philippines-led push for a review of its 1951 Mutual Defense Treaty with the United States, claiming that it is an effort to contain China's rise. The threat to use force is ever present. According to a Reuters news report: 'The push for clarity on Washington's commitment [to the treaty] comes amid a rapid build-up of Chinese maritime assets in contested areas of the South China Sea, including what the Philippines says is a militia disguised as a massive fishing fleet near Beijing's militarised manmade islands.'[2]

The vast majority of Chinese people, who have some knowledge of the recent troubles in Hong Kong involving the ruthless suppression by Chinese security forces of the democracy movement and the trashing of international agreements, nonetheless support China's intervention and cannot understand why the privileged people of that special province are not thankful to the party for the riches they enjoy. The Chinese people are proud that the State is taking back the South China Sea. Of course, the people do not want war, but if the State needs war to ensure their security, they will trust and support the State.

* * *

China understands deterrence and is not unhappy that information on its nuclear weapons program has been made public across the world. To deter a first strike by its enemies, China has to be capable of a credible second strike, and likely adversaries need to know this. Initially, the nation's nuclear force was focused on the US, but, thanks to their shared border, the Chinese have long considered Russia the most threatening enemy, despite the spring of friendship that bloomed at the time of the Ukraine War.

Until the Russians found themselves bogged down in Ukraine, they were prepared to say anything to encourage China to take on the US but were actually ambivalent about who would win. Russia simply wanted US power reduced across the world, particularly in the Baltic and within NATO. The economic synergies between Russia with its vast reserves of natural resources and China with its manufacturing power, plus the autocratic government systems of each nation, were, however, natural attractors. Declarations of everlasting friendship between Russia and China, and personally

At the Winter Olympics, early in 2022, President Xi Jinping and President Putin made declarations of everlasting friendship and loyalty – as Putin was positioning his troops to invade Ukraine. *(Alamy)*

between President Xi and President Putin, were made early in 2022 while President Xi was presiding over the Winter Olympics in China – and just as Putin was moving troops into the border area of Ukraine and issuing a series of demands to the US and NATO. After a post-Olympics summit, Russia and China released a joint statement warning Europe and the US that NATO forces should not approach the borders of the Russian Federation and asserting that Ukraine lay within Russia's sphere of influence.

When the mighty Russian army crossed Ukraine's borders on 24 February 2022 and attempted to decapitate the Ukraine government and so control the whole nation, as it had succeeded in doing in Georgia in 2004, most of the world expected a quick victory. But this time the decapitation strategy failed and left the conscript Russian army clumsily fighting on at least four fronts. There was a breakdown of logistical support for the masses of troops because the Russians had banked on a short, sharp campaign, and the West was astonished by the valour of the Ukrainian military and people fighting the Bear. The fact that the war turned out to be neither short nor sharp meant that NATO was able to ship weapons to Ukraine, including the most sophisticated anti-tank guided missiles and portable air-defence missiles, which, at least in the north and north-east of Ukraine, stopped the Russian army. This delay in a conclusion to the war also meant that the democratic nations of the world could not only put together the most daunting set of sanctions ever seen outside of the world wars but could also assess whether the sanctions were working or not, and then adjust them as required. As the Russian people started to feel the consequences of President Putin's rash actions on their standard of living, the Russian army reverted to a massive and indiscriminate use of firepower, the traditional floundering way of war for Russia. At the time of writing, the war grinds on with little sign of a victory for either side, or any kind of negotiated settlement. The question for the Western Pacific nations, and especially for Australia, is what lessons will China choose to learn from Ukraine in relation to the use of force?

The Russian attack on Ukraine has made the US starkly aware that it has at least two major enemies in the world, China and Russia. Of the two, China is still considered the most threatening in the medium to longer term, given its power in the Pacific. Russian aggression in Eastern Europe was always something the US hoped could be handled by Europe and NATO. During the Cold War, the US had accepted that it had to maintain armed forces capable of fighting and winning two major wars and one minor war simultaneously. But since the end of the Cold War in 1991, by the US government's own admission, its armed forces have been manned, equipped and funded to win only one major war, and to 'hold' in one minor war. After the Russian invasion of Ukraine, when the US cast its glance back to China, Taiwan and the Pacific, it found itself facing two enemies with a one-enemy military.

* * *

Despite its increasing influence on the global stage, not everything looks rosy for China. Annual economic metrics show that its growth has begun to slow, which is inevitable as it develops. China feels itself strategically encircled by the US, India, Japan and South Korea, and by new alliances such as AUKUS (the strategic agreement between Australia, the United Kingdom and the United States), and to some extent sees Australia as part of that threat. There is some argument that China might be reaching the peak of its power, which will decrease over time or at best plateau for an indefinite period.[3]

The question is whether this makes China more dangerous or less dangerous. Michael Beckley and Hal Brands write in *Foreign Affairs* magazine:

> *If there is a formula for aggression by a peaking power, China exhibits the key elements ... Beijing is a strong revisionist power that wants to remake the world, but it's time to do so is already running out. This realisation should not inspire complacency ... just the opposite. Once-rising powers frequently become aggressive when their fortunes fade and their enemies multiply. China is tracing an arc that often ends in tragedy: a dizzying rise followed by the spectre of a hard fall. Revisionist powers tend to become most dangerous when the gap between their ambitions and their capabilities start to look unmanageable. When a dissatisfied power's strategic window begins to close, even a low-probability lunge for victory may seem better than a humiliating descent. When authoritarian leaders worry that geopolitical decline will destroy their political legitimacy, desperation often follows.[4]*

If China has peaked as a power, what will it now do? Will this make it more dangerous, and how should the world react? These are critical questions for Australia and for our allies.

Few question China's worldwide ambitions, but in his book *Unrivaled: Why America Will Remain the World's Sole Superpower*, Michael Beckley certainly doesn't think China is in a position to dominate the world. Beckley, a fellow in the International Security Program at Harvard's Kennedy School, delves into the available economic, demographic and military data on the Chinese regime to determine whether it can really hope to become a global power in the same league as the US. His answer? Such a scenario is extremely unlikely. Rather than heading in the direction of rivalling the US, China is a rapidly ageing, inefficient, conflict-ridden and relatively poor country that simply is not on the road to seriously challenging the US's hegemony.[5]

A view like this, expressed in general terms, that China is not likely to threaten US dominance, is likely to be misunderstood. It allows us the luxury of reinforcing a strategy of hope that regional war will not occur. But this is not what Beckley is saying.

In the military, when we are planning for an uncertain future, we define the 'bounds of feasible planning'. Events that are within those bounds can be predicted with some degree of confidence and can thus be planned for. Events outside those bounds are so dependent on the success or failure of earlier events that, except in the most general sense, planning for them is impossible.

World dominance by China, as addressed by Beckley, I consider to be outside the bounds of feasible planning and will leave for others to examine. However, regional dominance by China, in my view, is well within such bounds and must be examined. It must form the contingency against which those involved in the region should plan. Regional war cannot be dismissed because at present China is not in a position to dominate the world.

Regardless of whether the world may consider that China's power is peaking and plateauing, a vital assumption made by Xi Jinping's administration is that China is on the way up the power ladder while America is on the way down. Daniel Russel, a top State Department official under President Obama, has said, 'The strongest driver of increased Chinese assertiveness is the conviction that the Western system, and the US in particular, is in decay.'[6] China may not be world-dominant yet, but it is quite capable of a regional test of strength in its own backyard. And if China is able to be dominant in the region, this might increase its view of whether or not it could ultimately be dominant across the world.

Furthermore, President Xi has been talking tough with regard to local geopolitics, as *Wall Street Journal* columnist Walter Russell Mead noted in October 2021:

Tension over Taiwan has been mounting for
months. In a major speech commemorating the
100th anniversary of the founding of the Chinese
Communist Party, delivered in Tiananmen Square
in July, [Xi Jinping] promised to 'utterly defeat' any
attempt toward Taiwanese independence ... Over the
weekend of China's Oct. 1 National Day, a record
149 Beijing military aircraft crossed into the island's
air-defense identification zone.[7]

To up the ante, Beijing hawks in the *Global Times* newspaper, the CCP's mouthpiece, have focused on the presence of a very small number of US troops in Taiwan involved in training the Taiwanese military. The paper's editor-in-chief referred to the presence of US troops in Taiwan as 'a red line that cannot be crossed' and warned that in the event of war in the Taiwan Strait, 'those US military personnel will be the first to be eliminated'.[8] The *Global Times* has also stated, in its attempts to keep the tensions high, that if Japan defends Taiwan, then China will make Japan an exception to its rule about never using nuclear weapons against a non-nuclear nation.[9]

What China says, even if it is through its *Global Times* mouthpiece, should not be dismissed as just rhetoric or paranoia. If you are paranoid – and China is exhibiting strong indications that it might be – it is not difficult to find people or organisations that look like they hate you and against which you eventually feel you should act. Even if this is rhetoric based on deep paranoia, there is no reason to disbelieve that at some stage it will develop into violent action. Statements such as this one from the *Global Times* must at least be a basis for future contingency planning.

China's paranoia is manifest at the moment in the expansion of its military to a historic level, and at a historic rate. The CCP has said exactly what it intends to do – in certain circumstances China will use military force – and it has made the judgment that it has the military power to act at any time. China can afford to focus its military plans on the island chains to its east; in contrast, its chief rival, the US, accepting the worldwide security responsibilities that have fostered a secure and prosperous world since 1945, must spread its military capability across the world. The key strategic question now is: if China has the military power to act, what exactly can it do, and when might it do it?

CHAPTER 4

IN THE GREY ZONE

At present, it is generally acknowledged that China is involved in what is known as grey-zone conflict. This is conflict above the level of normal competitive activities such as trade and lawful influence, but below the level of war. These grey-zone activities have consisted of punitive trade actions, irrational demands made through wolf-warrior diplomacy, unlawful influence over politicians and institutional leaders, intimidation of ethnic groups, denial of international law, physical occupation of disputed territory, militarisation of contested regional terrain, and general coercion, threats and bluster.

China has been making increasing use of *non*-military means of conflict, particularly coercive diplomacy and cyber-attacks. Australia has experienced more than its fair share of such activities, but we are not the only target. According to the Australian Department of Defence, over the past 10 years there have been 152 cases of such coercion affecting 100 governments and 52 companies, with an exponential increase in such tactics since 2019.[1]

It is not only the resources of China that can be brought to bear as this grey-zone conflict continues. China has so-called friends and, as mentioned earlier, Russia, as a main China ally and also a Pacific power, would like to see China diminish the power of the US in this or any part of the world, if for no other reason than it will distract the US from Russia's activities in Ukraine. We have not yet seen a major power, much less *two* major powers, conduct the highest level of cyber-attack possible on another country. The cyber-attacks by Russia on Ukraine have not been as disabling as predicted, and the reason for this may not be known for some time. But Russia and China combined have massive cyber influence, and their common friends, Iran and North Korea, are active in this field as well.

It is now widely known that in 2015 Russian hackers tunnelled deep into the computer systems of the US Democratic National Committee, and subsequent email leaks had a significant impact on US politics. But to interpret the impact of such activities as *only* political is to miss the bigger, more important story. In that same year, as David Sanger describes in his book *The Perfect Weapon: War, Sabotage, and Fear in the Cyber Age*, the Russians not only broke into networks at the White House, the State

Department and the US Joint Chiefs of Staff offices, but also placed implants in American electrical and nuclear facilities that potentially give them the power to switch off vast swathes of the country.[2]

This was the culmination of a decade of escalating digital sabotage among the world's powers, in which Americans and their allies became the collateral damage as China, Iran, North Korea and Russia battled in cyberspace to undercut one another in daily just-short-of-war conflict.[3] Prime Minister Scott Morrison indicated in June 2020, in a very public statement, that all levels of Australian government, critical infrastructure and the private sector were being targeted in a 'sophisticated state-based' cyber-attack, and confirmed it had been conducted by 'a sophisticated state-based cyber actor', assumed by commentators to be China.[4] In the past decade or so, cyber-attacks have displaced terrorism and North Korea's nuclear missiles in the public's mind as the most critical threat to Australia's vital interests.[5] The Coalition government reacted to this by progressively increasing Australia's offensive and defensive cyber capabilities and, in a massive leap forward, nearly doubled those capabilities through an AUD$10 billion investment over ten years in the 2022 budget.

China has long been known for attempting to steal intellectual property and industrial secrets through cyber intrusions. Chinese authorities and 'netizens' routinely conduct low-level attacks against information infrastructure: they silently penetrate systems, map their security and connections, and prepare for further penetrations in times of conflict. A recent shift, though, has been towards using cyber technology to inflict physical damage. In a notable recent example, China mounted a cyber campaign against India's electrical power grid to coincide with a clash between the two nations on the border in Ladakh.

Cyber technologies have given China some major advantages when undertaking coercive diplomacy, and its grey-zone activities can now have an impact on distant nations, not just those in its region. Chinese grey-zone activity even extends into space, where China has tested weapons and created significant debris fields that make some near-Earth orbits unusable. According to Bill Gertz in the *Washington Times*:

> *The PLA [People's Liberation Army] plans to use outer space to project power far from its shores and defeat adversaries, including the US, in a future conflict … Its space warfare arms, dubbed counter-space weapons, include a wide range of systems. The PLA has begun to transition the arms from testing to deployment. The weapons include ground-launched 'kinetic kill vehicles' – precision-guided missiles that slam into satellites at extremely high speeds. Other*

space weapons are orbiting robot killer satellites,
directed energy weapons, electronic jammers and
cyberwarfare capabilities.[6]

In July 2021, *The Australian* reported on assessments by UK and US military leaders that China and Russia are carrying out threatening actions against Western satellites daily, as part of a 'reckless' pattern of behaviour. According to General Sir Patrick Sanders of the UK's Strategic Command, Moscow has been manoeuvring satellites 'close to what they know is a sensitive or important satellite to us' to force a Western satellite to move to a less strategic area.

The Chief of the UK Air Staff, Air Chief Marshal Sir Mike Wigston, has stated that a Russian spy satellite has been gathering intelligence on commercial and military satellites.[7] Wigston said that the UK cannot yet see everything that Russia has been doing, but what they have been seeing is 'questionable'. Wigston also accused China of developing missiles to target satellites, laser-dazzle weapons to 'blind' targets, and electronic jammers. Further, Wigston revealed that Russian weapons can ram other satellites: they 'are practising against their own redundant satellites ... When we talk about reckless behaviour in space, these are the things we see.'[8] Wigston's assessment was complemented by reports from the Deputy Commander of US Space Command, Lieutenant General

John Shaw, who said: 'If we were in a potential conflict scenario, we would be relying on space, the United Kingdom would be relying on space. If the Chinese take out our space capabilities, it could affect our ability to wage war in the terrestrial domains.'[9]

The same military chiefs suggest that a future war would be won or lost in space, because the ability to destroy another country's satellites could have an immediately devastating effect. This is a critical judgment for these military leaders to make in this specialist area, and their views are doubtless well known to China. Given this, and the fact that Australia is part of the Five Eyes alliance, which shares intelligence between the US, the UK, Canada, New Zealand and Australia (a grouping commonly known as 'the Anglosphere'), any attack on a satellite belonging to one of the other four members of the alliance would have to be regarded as a direct threat to Australia.

* * *

China has also employed its maritime militia as part of its grey-zone activity. Properly known as the People's Armed Forces Maritime Militia (PAFMM), it is a very large, irregular force of fishing and other civilian boats controlled by the State. Some crew members are armed, but with concealed weapons. They are sometimes referred to as 'little blue men', a phrase borrowed from the militia forces used

A Philippine coastguard ship sails past a much larger Chinese coastguard ship off Scarborough Shoal, a triangular reef in the South China Sea that is claimed by the Philippines, China and Taiwan. *(Getty)*

by Russia during its 2014 occupation of parts of Ukraine, who were known as 'little green men'.[10]

China's maritime militia has been widely used to intimidate other nations when the use of identifiable military vessels might be too provocative. In 2012 the militia participated in China's illegal seizure of Scarborough Shoal from the Philippines. In 2014 it was used to repel Vietnamese ships from an oil rig that China had stationed near the contested Paracel Islands. And in 2015 the militia attempted to prevent a US destroyer from exercising its right to free passage in international waters, known by the US as a freedom-of-navigation operation or FONOPS, near an artificial island illegally constructed by China, called Subi Reef.

IN THE GREY ZONE

All these activities are clear signs that China wants to impose its will on other nations, but not through violence just yet – mainly because there is a chance of prevailing through other means. Grey-zone conflict is likely to increase in the short term. Possible activities include even more severe trade embargoes, unattributable biological attacks, anonymous cyber-attacks and mysterious interruptions to space-based capabilities.

But while China has achieved a number of objectives through grey-zone conflict, such as making the nine-dash line a realistic territorial boundary, this strategy is unlikely to bring about the main prizes of securing Taiwan and pushing the US out of the Western Pacific. China will need to do more to achieve those objectives, and we should be very concerned about that.

73

CHAPTER 5

WHERE AND WHEN?

The most obvious war scenario for Australians to consider is what is commonly called the Taiwan scenario.[1] Most commentators seem to misinterpret this scenario as one that is geographically limited to the region around the island of Taiwan and the Taiwan Strait, and concentrates on whether a Chinese invasion force could move across the strait by sea and air in order to invade, given Taiwan's defences and the ability of the US to intervene.[2] I am not saying that this scenario could never occur; what I am arguing is that it is dangerously simplistic and portrays Chinese strategists and tacticians as fools, which would be a silly assumption for planners to make.

If China were to move on Taiwan only, leaving US air and naval power in the Western Pacific untouched, it would risk a long and damaging counteraction by the US. Given time and the willingness of its allies, the US might be able to assemble its not insignificant regional military power and mount immediate and sizeable counterattacks from local US and allied bases. Then, over time, the US and its allies might be able to concentrate their world power by assembling additional forces in the region and apply that power against China. China might still be able to win this kind of limited D-Day-style Taiwan conflict, but absorbing US air and naval attacks over a period of time, as Saddam Hussein found out twice in Iraq, would involve enormous costs to its military and to its infrastructure on the mainland.

A more realistic option for China, which addresses both the Taiwan question and another of China's most important strategic objectives, the expulsion of US power from the Western Pacific, is the one I have presented as a hypothetical scenario in the prologue. If China could push US forces out of the region and deter them from attempting to approach its coastline, then China would become the dominant regional power. At the same time, this would simplify almost all the problems of 'reincorporating' Taiwan into the PRC.

If China decides to invade Taiwan and limits itself to that objective only, it will certainly attract the enmity of the US and the rest of the world, as well as military attacks from the US and others that have military forces in the region. But China might just consider, as Japan did at Pearl Harbor in 1941, that if you are going to be hated, it is worth going all the way and removing the regional ability of the US to use force against you. Then you can deal with Taiwan in any way you want, and it becomes irrelevant how much you are hated by the US – as long as the US does not use nuclear weapons.

Taiwan is important to China in a nationalistic sense because the CCP has staked its reputation on regaining its claimed lost province. To do this in the limited scenario most Australians think of as a Taiwan conflict, China needs either to so intimidate the US that it concedes regional power to China without fighting for Taiwan, or to entice US naval forces within the range of Chinese weapons so that they suffer significant casualties and the US then withdraws its surviving forces and removes its bases that sustain air and naval activities. To act so decisively, China would have to be as bold as the Japanese were at Pearl Harbor and take even more risks than them. For the Japanese it did not pay off. For the Chinese – who knows?

If China threatened Taiwan and the US was not able to resolve the situation in its own favour, then it would be a severe blow to US credibility and the region would perceive the US as a diminished power. If the US refused even to try to fight China because it did not believe its forces were strong enough, that would confirm US weakness to every regional nation. From the most recent statements of President Biden, it does not look as though the US is going to succumb peacefully and hand power to China without a fight of some kind.

An even worse result for regional stability, however, would be if the US tried to resolve a Taiwan scenario with force and was tactically defeated while Taiwan fell into China's hands. Then the US would be weakened militarily *and* in terms of prestige. This option could have frightening consequences for Australia.

There are other possible conflict scenarios – a Chinese attack on Japan's Senkaku Islands, or serious conflict on the China–India border, or conflict with Vietnam or the Philippines, for example. But if Australia was prepared for the Taiwan scenario as I have described it, and not as it is generally misinterpreted, then we would be prepared for all other non-nuclear scenarios. Or, if we discussed such a scenario and even then elected *not* to prepare and to take a risk, at least the magnitude of the risk would be understood by the Australian government and people.

Really, what we are doing here is trying to predict the future when almost nothing is out of the question. Sadly, if we have prepared for four options, the real world might still find a fifth.

If nothing is impossible, then China could continue on its current way, regularly rumbling about Taiwan and issuing threats to all and sundry, but not taking military or other actions that the international community would consider illegal. Life in Australia would not change much. China might increase or decrease its use of trade sanctions against Australian goods, leading us to complain to international bodies, but generally the situation would be manageable.

China could even be overtaken by a popular reaction to authoritarian rule. The Chinese people could rise up and democracy could break out, as it did in Eastern Europe in the 1990s, and after a period of internal violence this might bring about the demise of the CCP. China might become a normal nation, expressing its power in terms of international competition for trade and legitimate influence. China might even retain the CCP and become something like communist Vietnam: socialism or communism with a real Chinese face, not a CCP face.

China *could* decide to take military action that is geographically limited to the island of Taiwan. The naval component of China's invasion could be smashed as it set out from the Chinese coast by a conventional missile counterattack from US nuclear submarines lurking in the Taiwan Strait, and by Taiwanese US-supplied weapons. Meanwhile, the air element of China's invasion force could be shot out of the sky by Taiwan's air defences, backed up by US, Japanese and South Korean air attacks from still-intact bases in the region or from US carrier battle groups. The political ramifications of a failed invasion could bring down at least Xi Jinping if not the entire CCP.

Alternatively, on a dark night, China's military, led by an independently thinking general, might move against Xi, with a similar result for the CCP.

If China changes course as a result of any of the options given above, it might become even more authoritarian, if that is possible, or possibly even democratic, or revert to any of the many governance arrangements between those two extremes. If there is change in the governance of China, as there was in Indonesia and in Vietnam, and that change is for the better, the world might enjoy 10, 20 or 50 years before the question of Taiwan's independence or a regional war needs to be again addressed.

Or, perhaps China will remain the same aggressive actor on the international scene yet suddenly the US and its allies decide to change their own strategy, and *Xi* is the one surprised as strong allied forces are placed on the Taiwanese front line as a serious part of the everyday defence of that prosperous and democratic nation. (More on this in the next chapter.) No policy of strategic ambiguity there, and the next move would be up to China.

In the worst case, someone makes a mistake, or for some unfathomable reason one party initiates a nuclear strike. No one can predict where a nuclear exchange between China and the US would end, except to say the deaths would be well into the tens of millions and the world would never be the same again. Modern nuclear weapons with less fallout than their predecessors may not destroy the whole world, but the use by either side or both, and the consequences of such use, are almost beyond comprehension.

China, of course, might suddenly invade Taiwan in some way that we have not thought of, catching the rest of the world napping. US leadership is weak and vacillating, so Taiwan might be incorporated, leaving Australia and the world to wonder where in the waters of the Pacific the democratic nations of the world will draw the next line.

Or, of course, China may act as I have described in the prologue of this book. China may give no indication of its intentions and catch out US military forces in their peacetime deployments in a surprise attack. In a coordinated offensive over only a few hours, China could destroy US and allied nations' space resources, thus blinding the US and limiting its gathering of intelligence and passing of data so essential to modern military operations. It might launch a massive cyber-attack supported by its friends Russia, Iran and North Korea, thereby closing down infrastructure and communications across the world. It might destroy or re-route undersea cables, thus switching off or monitoring the internet, which is critical for passing encrypted military and government data around the world. And it may use its world-class rocket and missile force to attack local US air and naval bases as well as US Navy ships at sea, thus destroying US military power in the Western Pacific, after which it might make Taiwan an offer Taiwan cannot refuse.

Regardless of the many possible contingencies, it is prudent from a planning point of view for Australia to look at a situation that is as difficult as reality can produce, rather than one that comfortably matches our preconceived ideas. The tendency is to plan for the future war that we would *like* to fight, not the one that an adversary is likely to initiate. History is replete with examples of countries doing exactly that – preparing for the war they wanted to fight, and not the one that an enemy was able to fight.

* * *

For Australians to assess whether we are prepared for the Taiwan scenario as I have outlined it, it is important that we understand how and where such a war would occur, which requires us to look more closely at the geography of the area.

The Western Pacific, where I believe this war could be fought, is part of what is now called, in a geostrategic sense, the Indo-Pacific. Until recently, the term used was 'Asia-Pacific' but the need to consider the area from the Middle East all the way to the US west coast – covering the Indian Ocean as well as the Pacific Ocean – as a single strategic entity, means the term Indo-Pacific is now used widely, even by the US military, who changed the name of their Pacific Command to the Indo-Pacific Command. 'Indo-Pacific' was

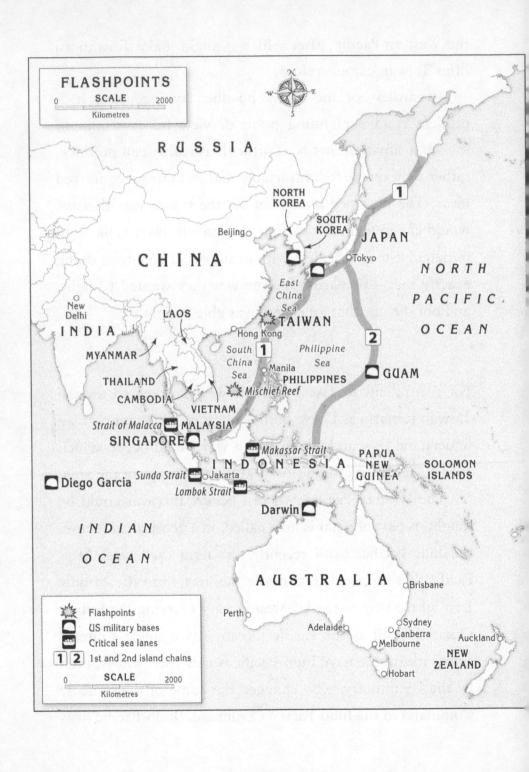

SCALE
0   2000
Kilometres

RUSSIA

NORTH
KOREA

SOUTH
KOREA

Beijing

CHINA

JAPAN

Tokyo

New
Delhi

INDIA

LAOS

MYANMAR

THAILAND

CAMBODIA

VIETNAM

Hong Kong

TAIWAN

East
China
Sea

NORTH

PACIFIC

OCEAN

South
China
Sea

Philippine
Sea

Manila

PHILIPPINES

Mischief Reef

GUAM

Strait of Malacca   MALAYSIA

SINGAPORE

Makassar Strait

PAPUA
NEW
GUINEA

SOLOMON
ISLANDS

Diego Garcia

Sunda Strait   Jakarta

INDONESIA

Lombok Strait

Darwin

INDIAN

OCEAN

AUSTRALIA

Brisbane

Perth

Adelaide

Sydney
Canberra

Melbourne

Auckland

NEW
ZEALAND

Hobart

Flashpoints
US military bases
Critical sea lanes
1 2 1st and 2nd island chains

SCALE
0   2000
Kilometres

a term first used by Australian strategists because Australia borders both the Pacific and Indian oceans and has an understanding of how the two oceans are linked in terms of trade and strategic interests.

The Western Pacific is a small part of the Pacific Ocean and consists of an awful lot of water and some major island chains, including Japan, the Philippines and New Guinea, many smaller islands and the coast of much of South-east Asia.

Among the smaller islands out to the east are the US-controlled Mariana Islands, which include the separate territories of the Northern Mariana Islands and Guam, where there are massive US air and naval bases and armouries; the Federated States of Micronesia; and the Marshall Islands, site of a US naval base on Kwajalein. There is a US Air Force base on Wake Island, and additional US bases may be established on Palau and Manus Island and even in Australia in the future. These mid-ocean islands played a vital role for both sides in World War II.

Closer to China's coast, in Japan, there is the Okinawa marine base and Iwakuni marine aviation base, with naval forces at Atsugi, Okinawa, Yokosuka, Sasebo and Misawa, plus US Air Force bases at Kadena, Misawa and Yokota, outside Tokyo. South Korea has several bases (Kunsan, Osan, Yongsan, Chinhae Navy Base and a number of US Army bases and camps) and of course a permanent deployment of US troops.

Far out in the Pacific, in Hawaii, lies the US Joint Base Pearl Harbor–Hickam, one of many in Hawaii, and far to the west, off the coast of India, there is a logistics base and a base for longer-range US bombers on Diego Garcia.

The China Seas (East and South) define the Chinese continental littoral, lying between the Chinese coast and Japan, the Philippines and the Malay Peninsula and extending eastward as far as the island of New Guinea. Within and beyond the Chinese littoral are three island chains that are particularly important to visualising a future war.

The first island chain is linked by China to the historical 'nine-dash line', discussed in Chapter 1, and runs from Russia's Kamchatka Peninsula to the Malay Peninsula. It consists of the Kurils in Russia, parts of the Japanese Archipelago, including the Ryukyu Islands, Taiwan, the Northern Philippines and Borneo. It also includes small islands within the Spratly and Paracel island groups that have been stolen and militarised by China, specifically four main militarised island bases and approximately 16 lesser islands, reefs or artifices on which radar and communications bases have been built. The first island chain is China's littoral, and if you elect to fight China in this area, you fight on China's chosen battlefield, with China holding all the advantages.[3]

The second island chain stretches from the main Japanese islands to well east of the Philippines, touching Guam, then swings west and south towards the Indonesian territory of West Papua.

The third island chain, a term rarely used, starts imprecisely in the vicinity of Alaska, crosses the Pacific to Hawaii and then runs down into the South Pacific.

Depending on where you stand, these island chains can be defensive as well as offensive. China experts Toshi Yoshihara and James R. Holmes wrote in 2018:

> *If anything, Chinese strategists see [the first island chain] as an American defence perimeter meant to channel, constrict and perhaps even block Chinese sea and air movements along the Asian seaboard and from the China Seas into the Western Pacific. If so, it is a hostile fortification to be punctured, not a friendly fortification to be defended.*[4]

Whether these island chains, the first and second in particular, are defensive or offensive in any future war will depend on who fortifies them first, when they are fortified and for what purpose. If Chinese forces can be rapidly located in small groups at key locations, particularly the land edges of sea straits, with anti-ship missiles to dominate passages between the islands, then China can push its defence and warning screen out another 1000 to 1500 kilometres. This would give the Chinese an immense advantage, allowing them to hold a US fleet even further out from its optimal weapons and aircraft ranges. Conversely, if US forces were able to be deployed first and hold similar positions with similar weapons (which, as we'll see, now appears to be part of the developing US operational concept), then the US could stop the Chinese from deploying their surface fleet from Chinese bases and seas to the second island chain, should it want to do so.[5]

Though technological advances may mean we now live in a 'shrinking' world, one of the toughest challenges in facing down China remains the tyranny of distance in the Indo-Pacific. This is illustrated when we look at the unrefuelled ranges of certain aircraft and the ranges of common cruise missiles as being in the vicinity of 1000 to 1500 kilometres. These are relevant for the tactical fight, but the distances for strategic reinforcement are even more daunting. Just look at the distances to Taiwan (Taipei) from various US bases: from Guam, 2750 kilometres; from Okinawa, 650 kilometres; from Tokyo, 2100 kilometres; from Seoul, 1485 kilometres; from Alaska, 7505 kilometres; from Diego Garcia, 6422 kilometres; and from Honolulu, 8114 kilometres.

* * *

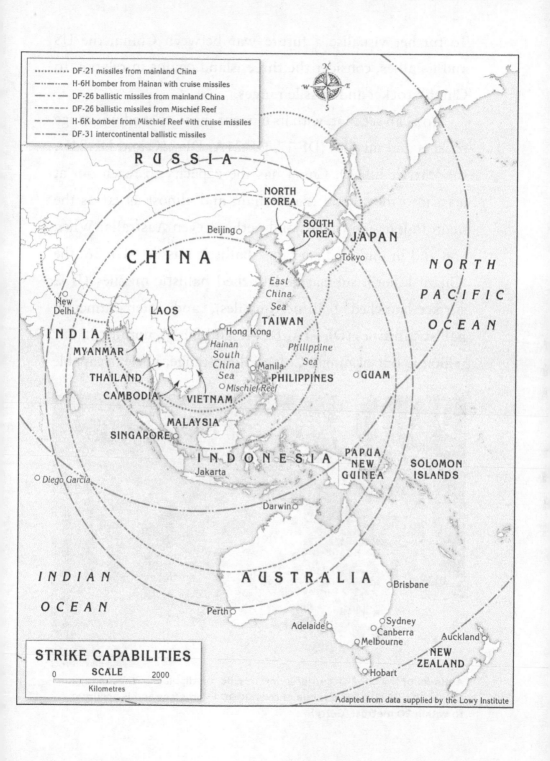

Legend:
- ·········· DF-21 missiles from mainland China
- - - - - - H-6H bomber from Hainan with cruise missiles
- — · — · DF-26 ballistic missiles from mainland China
- — ·· — ·· DF-26 ballistic missiles from Mischief Reef
- — — — H-6K bomber from Mischief Reef with cruise missiles
- — · — · DF-31 intercontinental ballistic missiles

RUSSIA

NORTH KOREA
SOUTH KOREA
JAPAN
Beijing
Tokyo
CHINA
East China Sea
NORTH
New Delhi
LAOS
TAIWAN
PACIFIC
INDIA
Hong Kong
Philippine Sea
OCEAN
MYANMAR
Hainan
South China Sea
Manila
THAILAND
PHILIPPINES
GUAM
CAMBODIA
VIETNAM
Mischief Reef
MALAYSIA
SINGAPORE
INDONESIA
PAPUA NEW GUINEA
SOLOMON ISLANDS
Jakarta
Diego Garcia
Darwin
INDIAN
AUSTRALIA
Brisbane
OCEAN
Perth
Sydney
Adelaide
Canberra
Melbourne
Auckland
NEW ZEALAND
Hobart

STRIKE CAPABILITIES

SCALE
0   2000
Kilometres

Adapted from data supplied by the Lowy Institute

To further visualise a future war between China, the US and its allies, consider the three island chains in relation to China's rocket and missile ranges.

You can see that, with its current short- to medium-range rockets and missiles (DF-17, DF-21A, DF-21C and DF-21D, the 'carrier killer'), China has the capacity to reach out at least into the second island chain and almost as far as the main Indonesian islands and perhaps even Australia. When you add in intermediate-range ballistic missiles (DF-26, the 'Guam killer'), submarine-launched ballistic missiles (JL-2 surface-launched ballistic missiles), and intercontinental ballistic missiles (DF-31A, DF-41 and DF-5), nothing in our region is out of range. Chinese long-range, nuclear-capable

A model of the DF-21D 'carrier-killer' missile, on display in Nanchang, China. The DF-21D has a range of over 2000 kilometres and is accurate to within 20 metres. *(Getty)*

bombers may have a reach of 9000 kilometres, according to some reports, though the reality is probably closer to half that range.[6]

China has the most active and diverse ballistic missile development program in the world. It is continually upgrading its missile force in terms of numbers, types and capabilities, modernising its intercontinental ballistic missiles, and developing multiple independently targetable re-entry and manoeuvring vehicles that can dodge missiles sent to intercept them. China has also begun deploying a new fleet of nuclear ballistic missile submarines. Short- to medium-range cruise and ballistic missiles form a critical part of what China calls its regional anti-access and area-denial capability, a term used to indicate that China can keep US forces out of its 'area' – that is, its littoral and at least the first island chain. For example, the 2000-kilometre-range DF-17 rocket can move towards a target at Mach 10 – some 12,200 kilometres per hour. A moving US aircraft carrier would be unlikely to evade such a missile or to survive a direct hit and a US base hit by several of these missiles would be taken out of action for days or even weeks.

China is keen to let the world know it has developed this advanced and powerful weaponry, a product of widespread theft of intellectual property, excellent Chinese innovation (especially in copying weapons) and the allocation of resources that an authoritarian state can make in the areas of technology and industry. To this end, China's air force released a video in September 2020 showing H-6 bombers making simulated strikes on a runway that looked like Andersen Air Force Base on Guam, a key staging area for US support for Taiwan.[7] According to Sampson Ellis, the CCP's *Global Times* reported that China's intermediate ballistic missiles, such as the DF-26, could take out American bases while China's air defences shot down incoming US aircraft, rockets and missiles. In August 2020, China fired four test missiles into the South China Sea that it is assumed would be capable of destroying US bases and aircraft carriers.[8]

The intermediate-range DF-26 is often showcased during military parades in Beijing, for example at the seventieth anniversary of the PRC's founding in October 2019. Since the DF-26 can be armed with both nuclear and conventional warheads, arms-control experts worry that any sign China is preparing to fire one could trigger a pre-emptive US nuclear strike – potentially leading to an uncontrollable conflict.[9]

Whether China will use these weapons to achieve its twin aims of reducing US power in the Pacific and reincorporating Taiwan, and *how* they will be used, have become key questions.

* * *

Another essential question for Australians to consider is the timing of any potential war. My estimate is that conflict over Taiwan could occur at any time within the next three to five years. This was originally based on my expectation that President Biden, when he was elected, would raise US military spending and it would take three to five years for this to significantly increase US military power. If China saw that its window of opportunity was closing, it might precipitate aggressive CCP action to achieve its strategic aims before US forces could grow in strength. Under the Biden administration, however, despite the tough talk, and based on the 2021–22 US defence budget, there is no indication that a significant increase in US military power is to occur before the next election; in fact, US support for the Ukraine War may mean that, overall, US military power diminishes in the very short term. This may make China think twice about the use of force, and delay any such move, or precipitate an early move. The unpredictability means that the worst-case scenario – any time in the next three to five years – must still be the basis of prudent planning.

The timing of such a war might also depend on how ready China is, and how unprepared and weak China perceives the US and Taiwan to be. Authoritarian governments have a distinct advantage in being able to provide resources for their military without having to consider the will of the people to the same extent as a democratic country.

As Reuters reported, on 6 October 2021, Taiwan's defence minister Chiu Kuo-cheng voiced his opinion that China already has the capacity to invade his country:

> *Chiu said China already has the ability to invade Taiwan and it will be capable of mounting a 'full-scale' invasion by 2025. 'By 2025, China will bring the cost and attrition [of an invasion] to its lowest. It has the capacity now, but it will not start a war easily, having to take many other things into consideration.'*[10]

China might act in the aftermath of another failure, such as was recently seen in Afghanistan, or take advantage of a conflict that diverts US military attention to a place like the Black Sea, the Baltic, the Persian Gulf or, of course, Ukraine.

* * *

The bottom line is that China should not be underestimated. It has the world's largest army, navy, militia, non-nuclear rocket force (referred to as sub-strategic) and homeland air defence. It has not been involved in a war requiring sophisticated joint warfighting since 1979, when it arrogantly attacked Vietnam to teach that country a lesson and was soundly beaten and humiliated. That failure is often seen as highly relevant when assessing the modern warfighting capability of China and is often used to dismiss China as a threat. But the US and most of its allies have also not been involved in the kind of war that might be fought in the Western Pacific as portrayed here. The US has not fought a peer adversary since Japan in World War II, or China in Korea in 1950. The US and its allies will have some advantage in joint warfighting from experience gained in a series of recent counter-insurgency and counter-terrorist wars, but that advantage should not be overstated in relation to the kind of war China could fight on its littoral and in the island chains.

It would appear that, following a century of shame forced on it by its own weakness and the aggression of the colonising world, this time around China has noticed what strategy and tactics are all about. China is by no means militarily perfect and does have its vulnerabilities. But no Australian should ever think that US military power is infinite compared with China's, as we have grown to believe over the last 75 years. No Australian should think that as a Taiwan scenario starts to unfold, our nation need not prepare. And if the US is defeated in a fight with China or decides to not engage and so surrenders its credibility and influence in our region without a fight, no Australian should ever think that the implications for Australia will not be immense.

US Iraq War commander David Petraeus's famous comment 'Tell me how this ends' is as relevant here as anywhere.[11]

CHAPTER 6

THE RESPONSE: THE US AND ITS ALLIES

In 1941, the world was aware that Japan was on the verge of military action in the Pacific. Knowing that Japan had only one year's worth of oil reserves, the US had cut it off from its oil supplies because of Japan's aggression towards China. In order to deter military action on Japan's part, in mid-1940 the US had moved a major part of its Pacific fleet from other bases to Pearl Harbor, thus providing the Japanese with a clear Pacific target.

Not only did the US arrange its fleet as a target in an eye-pleasing manner in Pearl Harbor, but it also lined up its aircraft on Hawaii's airfields to be destroyed in detail. It was only luck that saved US aircraft carriers from destruction as well. And all of this occurred at a time when the US thought it knew exactly where the Japanese fleet was, thanks to access to some of Japan's secret coded messaging.

The very day after the infamous 7 December 1941 attack on Pearl Harbor, the Japanese attacked and destroyed US air forces in the Philippines while they were still lined up wingtip to wingtip. And just days later, to top it all off, the Japanese sank two of the best battleships the British had off Malaya, with losses in the thousands.

The assumption that we will act logically and our enemies will act stupidly is a very dangerous one indeed. And it is certainly not proven by history.

Could it happen again?

Arrogantly disregarding the Taiwan scenario as a geographically limited war between China and Taiwan is reminiscent of the West's attitude to Japan before World War II. An unwillingness on the part of US and allied planners and politicians to accept that China will use all the weapons systems that it has spent decades developing against US bases and naval units in China's backyard is a similarly appalling error of judgment.

The US and its allies must not make the Pearl Harbor error again. Only by understanding the likely nature of war with China in the Pacific, and only by planning for the worst while hoping for the best can they deter a devastating conflict or, if deterrence fails, as it does so often, have some chance of surviving.

* * *

Understanding what kind of conflict may lie ahead is particularly important for Australia, given that we are now more vulnerable than we have been since the 1930s, years before Pearl Harbor. It is not only the Chinese we should be concerned about, but also the willingness of our major ally, the US, to confront them. Even if the Americans *are* willing to confront China when the time comes, will they and their allies be able to harness enough military force to prevail?[1]

The question arises time and time again: if there is not a high level of confidence in the US that it could be successful in even a simple Taiwan scenario, then why would it commit itself militarily? *Not* stepping in to defend Taiwan, having provided the Taiwanese with weapons for decades and warned China against a military solution, would represent a serious lessening of US influence in the region, and would be a severe blow to Australia's security.

To deter a foe, a military force cannot just posture, it must be able to fight and so impose an unacceptable potential cost on its adversary. If the US government is not able to look its allies in the eye and say that a coalition the US might propose to lead has at least a fair chance of success, why would the US propose such a coalition, and why would anyone join it? In particular, why would Australia commit to such a deployment given our paucity of military forces? And why would *any* coalition partner commit to such a serious undertaking unless they had a say in the strategy to achieve success?

Where in the vast Pacific waters would we draw the line on China's power, if we do not draw it around Taiwan? Yet, Taiwan's external supporters must be prepared to back Taiwan with the lives of their sons and daughters, because that will be the cost. For most countries, and particularly the US, at this stage that is a politically difficult notion. The US is war weary after years of fighting in the Middle East and believes that it was left unfairly by its allies to carry most of the cost of those long years of war. Its involvement in support of Ukraine against Russia is yet another drain on US attention and on US weapons. The last thing it wants to do after its recent experiences in Iraq and in Afghanistan and its ongoing experience in eastern Europe is to take over the defence of Taiwan.

As was explained earlier, it is traditional in intelligence circles when assessing possible adversaries to look at both intent and capability. This is a very powerful intelligence framework. Despite the importance of the US to Australian security, I don't believe that we have looked at our great ally, our great friend, in those terms with sufficient scrutiny.

Who cares how big and aggressive China becomes in our region if the US is powerful enough and willing enough to lead its allies in deterring Chinese actions, militarily or otherwise? Yet since the end of the Cold War in the early

1990s, even as the US continues to accept its worldwide military responsibilities, to expand on an earlier point, its effective military power has reduced by a frightening 30 to 50%. This is clear from its own National Security and Defense strategies.[2]

As early as 1998, the US National Security Strategy illustrated this frightening decline in US power and the magnitude of the task of recovery. Referring to its plan, for obvious reasons, as the 'two and a half war strategy', it stated: 'We must maintain superior military forces at the level of readiness necessary to effectively deter aggression, conduct a wide range of peacetime activities and smaller-scale contingencies ['half-wars'], and, preferably in concert with regional friends and allies, win two overlapping major theatre [sic] wars.'[3]

US war weariness from winning the Cold War and from the long inconclusive wars in the Middle East manifested in a period of defence budgets that were significantly less than was necessary to maintain US forces as superior to their peer adversaries. Critics of US defence spending asked for and received a 'peace dividend' – sadly the peace was ephemeral. During the first two decades of this century, US defence budgets were in the vicinity of US$700 billion per year (in today's dollars). A better comparison during that period was that the budgets were between 3% and 4.9% of GDP. During the peak of the Cold War the US spent

5.9% of its GDP on defence. This amount goes up and down depending on whether the cost of the current war is included in the total figure. In 2005, as the Iraq War was increasing in magnitude, the budget was US$493 billion, which was 4.09% of US GDP. When both wars in Iraq and Afghanistan were running down, President Obama inherited a budget of US$738 billion (4.9% of GDP) and then ran it down to US$646 billion (3.31% of GDP). The first budget signed into law by President Biden at the end of 2021 was US$777 billion. What suffered most from these budget cuts was not just personnel numbers, but investment in the most modern weapons, aircraft, ships and equipment. It is often stated that the US spends more on defence than the next at least 16 countries combined, but, although it is a staggering amount of money, fundamentally what the US spends on defence is irrelevant. This is because money spent on defence is an *input*. As the Ukrainians are showing the world, what is important is not what a defence force *has*, but what it can do, what it gets for what it spends – its *output*, in other words. And the most important output of a defence force is its ability to win wars. For this is the definitive judgment and the military is required by US law to state this judgment once every two years in its National Security Strategy.

By 2018, and as a comparison to its judgment in 1998, reflecting both the further demise of US military power and the growth of military might in China, Russia, Iran and North Korea, the US National Security Strategy only required that 'in wartime, the fully mobilised Joint Force will be capable of: defeating aggression by a major power; deterring opportunistic aggression elsewhere; and disrupting imminent terrorist and WMD [weapons of mass destruction] threats'. Critics of this strategy call this a 'one-and-a-half-war strategy'.

If, in the period from 1998 to today, the effective military capability of the mighty US has decreased from being able to win two and a half wars simultaneously, to being able, once fully mobilised, to win one major war and maybe hold in another (half) war, then Australian intelligence organisations had better start paying very close attention to the friend on whom we depend so entirely for our security. Australia needs to wake up to the fact that US military power is not infinite, and may become still weaker through budgetary decisions, industrial limitations and waning intent.

Australia should study the US to the same extent as I hope we study our potential adversaries. Not because the US is likely to become an adversary, but because as a dependent nation we cannot afford to misread either US intent (which is hard) or capability (which is relatively easy). At present it seems we read neither in a formal way.

We should watch very closely the budget decisions that the US makes, and carefully assess the implications for

Australia. We should be very sensitive to a US that is tired of war, that sees most of its allies free-riding on the US, and to any ally that talks of smaller defence budgets. And we need to know what a substantially smaller US defence budget would look like, because for Australians, that is the trillion-dollar question. The US decision about whether to support Taiwan will be based on a judgment as to how successful it is likely to be *at a reasonable cost*.

The issue of the defence budget was recently taken up by US Congressional Budget Office (CBO) analysts in a report that looked at how a smaller defence budget could be realised with a cut of $1 trillion over the 10 years from 2021 to 2031. This could be achieved, the authors wrote, 'by phased budget cuts over the first five years ... and growth with the rate of inflation thereafter', which could yield a 2031 defence budget 'about 15 percent smaller than DoD's [the Department of Defense's] 2022 funding request'.

Three very confusing options were proposed, none of which really looked at whether the US could win or lose a war or wars against a peer adversary. The first was called 'Proportional Reductions' and is essentially 'deterrence by denial', which involves 'denying or reversing military gains in regional conflicts', and eventually reducing personnel numbers by 20%. Option 2 is called 'Coalition Defense', described as 'deterrence through punishment', which 'would call for reductions in conventional forces, such as brigade combat teams and fighter aircraft, and increases in long-range strike capabilities, such as cruise missiles, anti-ship missiles, and air-defense missiles'. The third option is called 'Command of the Commons' and emphasises 'freedom of navigation in sea, air, and space around the world' and 'avoids the use of large ground forces to seize and hold territory in regional conflicts in favour of engaging enemies at standoff ranges'.

'Although substantial,' the CBO report continues, 'a reduction that reached 15 percent by 2031 would be smaller than both the 1990s' budget reductions (a 30 percent decline in annual budgets between 1988 and 1997) and the 18 percent decline in annual budgets between 2012 and 2015 that followed enactment of the Budget Control Act of 2011'.[4]

It appears that this report has had little impact, but just the fact that it is out there illustrates how reluctant the current US administration is to spend big on defence. Since 9/11, the US has been continually at war in the Middle East, with only limited support from its allies, and simultaneously challenged by an empowered China, Russia, North Korea and Iran. To increase spending, groups within Congress are trying to add US$24 billion to a Pentagon budget proposal that far exceeds US spending at the peak of the Korean and Vietnam wars, probably because the cost of both volunteer personnel and state-of-the-art equipment today is many times more than it was during the 1950s and 60s. The Congressional Budget Office analysis, so say the opponents of large defence spending, 'offers an opportunity to step back and take a closer look at how much is actually necessary to protect the US and its allies … At a time when the greatest risks to our lives and livelihoods are not military in nature, saving a trillion dollars that could be devoted to preventing pandemics, addressing climate change, or reducing racial and economic injustice is no small matter.'[5]

This statement is realistic in relation to the many challenges facing the US, but it is totally unrealistic to ignore the one big challenge to US power, and that is an aggressive China. The ramifications for Australia if the US fails to stabilise its own power in our region are immense.

In terms of potential adversaries, China, of course, is not the only focus. The 2018 US National Defense Strategy, which is a subset of the US National Security Strategy previously described, identified five major military threats for the US: China, Russia, Iran, North Korea, and terrorist groups. Since 2018, each of those threats has only grown more serious.

The much-publicised 'Pivot to Asia' during the Obama and Trump administrations was a policy to recognise the importance of Asia and in particular China, compared to Europe and the Middle East, for US diplomacy and the US military. Despite much talk, the policy pivot produced very little in terms of diplomacy and even less in terms of moving military resources to the Pacific. At the same time, there are encouraging signs that other parts of the US government are homing in on China in particular. One area of national security that is, critically, focusing on China is intelligence. In October 2021, the security website *Defense One* reported:

> *The CIA's new China Mission Center sends a clear signal to the intelligence community that it's time to shift its focus to near-peer competitors after 20 years of tracking terrorist threats, two analysts said. The center is part of the administration's broader effort to pivot the national security community's focus towards competition with great powers, such as China, and away from the counterterrorism operations that dominated the past two decades, including the war in Afghanistan that ended this summer. CIA Director William Burns announced on Thursday that the new China Mission Center will bring together capabilities from around the agency to better respond to the threat posed by Beijing.*[6]

The next US National Security Strategy is due and preliminary documents have been published. The full and final version was to have been out early in 2022, but there is a history of this important document being outpaced and delayed by the fast-moving real world and, in this case, probably the situation with Russia, Ukraine and NATO has impacted on the policy writers. As governments slowly recognise the importance of the threat from China, despite not yet taking significant action to counter it, it is ironic that four experts on the website *War on the Rocks* refer to the not yet completed National Security Strategy and write:

> *The strategy should acknowledge that China has the world's largest standing army, navy, coast guard, maritime militia, and sub-strategic missile force. But China's advantages are not only quantitative.*
>
> *As the likely home team in a confrontation with the United States, the People's Liberation Army has pursued capabilities specifically designed to frustrate the US military's ability to project power into the Western Pacific. The Defense Department's own military power report on China judges that this strategy has placed the Chinese military qualitatively ahead of the US military in land-based missiles and integrated air defenses, including new technologies such as hypersonic and directed-energy weapons. In other areas like AI [artificial intelligence] and energy storage, Beijing is exploiting its policy of military–civil fusion in innovation to gain an edge on US forces.*

The US military is emerging from a decade of
delayed modernization and insufficient funding,
whereas China grew its defense spending by at least
8% a year for the last decade.[7]

As this article suggests, and to repeat a point made earlier, the US is surfacing from decades of war in the Middle East with worn-out equipment, understandably having allocated a lot of its funding to 'today's wars' rather than investing in the future. During the Iraq War, for instance, Secretary of Defense Bob Gates wanted more drones to carry on the day-to-day fight in Iraq and found himself in conflict with the US Air Force, which wanted to continue building the fighters and bombers that it thought would be needed in the future. Gates sacked the chief of the US Air Force and restricted the production of aircraft such as the stealth F-22 fighter and the B-21 bomber, in order to build the drones and other aircraft he needed. The result was that only a limited number of the extraordinary F-22s were built and the B-21 is still not in production. The impact of diverted spending and focus will be felt for a long time to come. The likely war with China, if it is ever fought by weapons of this type, is going to be fought by a very small number of modern stealth fighters, but mainly by US fighters and bombers that are 20 to 30 years old.

The result of all this is that the US will not be able to marshal sufficient military power to deter China in the

Western Pacific, possibly for years. A University of Sydney study warned in 2019 that America 'no longer enjoys military primacy' over China and that US bases, air strips and ports in the region 'could be rendered useless by precision strikes in the opening hours of a conflict'.[8]

Nor should the US expect much help from its current regional allies. It doesn't appear that nations in the Western Pacific or the Indo-Pacific have the attitude towards mutual defence that was prevalent in devastated Europe after 1945, when NATO was formed. Such a binding defence alliance is unlikely in the Western Pacific. South Korea will always be too consumed by the threat from North Korea's massive land forces to undertake any large-scale manoeuvres that take its forces too far away from its own northern border.

Japan is changing in its attitude to the constitutional limitations imposed on it by Article 9 of its post-war constitution, which prohibits anything but military action in self-defence, and is now at least talking about pre-emptive strikes on adversary bases that may threaten it. Japan has made the significant declaration that an independent and free Taiwan is so important for Japanese security that it is to be regarded as an area covered by Japan's self-defence. This is still a far cry from Japan deploying its very capable military forces beyond its home islands to assist US forces in the seas around Taiwan. And, of course, Russia also represents a threat to Japan, which claims sovereignty over the Kuril Islands, occupied by Russia since 1945. This threat may, however, have decreased with the Ukraine War, which has forced Russia to move significant military forces from its eastern provinces to more central positions closer to Ukraine.

Vietnam is in conflict with China over a number of issues, particularly its maritime borders, and has suffered frequent Chinese intrusions. Vietnam's military today is not the military that defeated France, the US and China in the past, and as well as sharing a land border with China, which is a continuing threat, Vietnam has a navy and an air force which are small and totally outdated.

In our world, it is dangerous to be considered weak. If you are perceived by an adversary as weak, or you are in fact weak, especially with regard to conventional (non-nuclear) forces, and you are one of the nine countries in the world with nuclear weapons, you might face a dilemma. Because your conventional forces are weak, you may be tempted to consider using nuclear weapons, not just as a deterrent but in desperation. President Obama was considering declaring a 'no first use' nuclear policy for the US, and it seemed that the Biden administration was also considering such a policy.

Many US allies have found the idea of a 'no first use' policy by the US hard to accept. The US nuclear umbrella was something that emerged during the Cold War and is still seen as a guarantee that the US, as a nuclear-weapons state,

THE RESPONSE: THE US AND ITS ALLIES

will defend certain non-nuclear allied states, to discourage them from developing their own nuclear weapons. It is commonly said to apply to Australia, NATO, Japan and South Korea. Japan has been threatened with nuclear attack by China if it becomes involved in defending Taiwan, so for Japan this is a real issue.[9]

The US has historically maintained a policy of ambiguity about whether it would carry out a first strike with nuclear weapons, but the new policy that was being contemplated would expressly rule it out. According to Senator Jim Risch of Idaho: 'It gives more comfort to the enemy that they can plan an attack and do whatever they want to and not worry about us [carrying out] a first strike ... Nobody wants to use a first strike, but there are scenarios where you can imagine a first strike, and the best thing you can do is keep [adversaries] off balance.'[10] One of the very few upsides of the appalling Ukraine War, apart from the sanctions and the increase in readiness and armaments within NATO, is that President Biden has now stated that, given the repeated threats of the use of nuclear, biological and chemical weapons by Russia against Ukraine, the US will not adopt a 'no first use' nuclear policy as part of the US Nuclear Posture Review.

Meanwhile, to overcome at least the perception of weakness, the US is considering a very different policy to deter Chinese and Russian aggression. The four experts from *War on the Rocks* quoted earlier advocate that the US should establish a 'strengthened forward defense posture' in vital regions – that is, locating forces permanently, especially in the Indo-Pacific, rather than having to deploy them over very long distances in a period of tension or war.

The idea of a 'strengthened forward defense posture' is a complicated concept and is military-speak to explain that in the Pacific, Europe and South Korea, it has been the normal state of affairs that not all the US forces needed to fight a war are based close to where the war might be fought, in the so-called theatre. Instead, most of the forces required are located in the continental US, which is the source of manpower, equipment and training facilities and where it is normally less expensive to maintain large forces. Only a smaller number of troops are deployed permanently close to the various likely war theatres. In previous theatres such as Europe, South Korea and the Middle East, it was not uncommon to find that the forward deployed troops numbered in the order of perhaps 30,000 to 50,000, a relatively small number, and the troops that were deployed from their home bases once tension increased or war broke out numbered as many as several hundred thousand.

So, if tension increases or actual war breaks out, the very large forces have to be deployed from the US to the theatre where the war is occurring. It can be a very long and complicated process to move what might be hundreds of thousands of troops, with their equipment, vehicles, ships and aircraft, literally from one side of the world to the other. It might be slightly easier to deploy combat aircraft or warships than it is to deploy large numbers of soldiers, but there is still a delay and in the case of a surprise attack, or a fait-accompli attack, as it is sometimes called, this delay can be disastrous. And, of course, while those forces are being deployed in troop ships or transport aircraft, they may be vulnerable to being attacked if the enemy has the capability to do so.

The US used to practise the deployment of forces from the continental US to either South Korea or Europe in massive exercises every few years, so that it was confident it could readily carry out such a deployment and potential

US soldiers from Camp Humphreys in Pyeongtaek, South Korea, on exercises in May 2022. Camp Humphreys is the largest overseas US military base, with a population of more than 45,000. *(Getty)*

enemies could also see that it was feasible. The balance between the smaller permanently forward-deployed troops and the larger number of those to be deployed into the theatre when necessary was based on risk assessments conducted regularly.

When the threat from Russia against Europe was very high or the threat from North Korea was more than the South Korean army was capable of handling, the majority of US troops required to win the war in Europe or the Korean peninsula were actually stationed in the relevant theatre. As the threat diminished, or the local forces were assessed as adequate, the bulk of US troops were sent home and only a small force was kept 'forward-deployed', as the military says.

One function of the permanently forward-deployed US forces was to act as a tripwire. That is, if an enemy invaded the country or area concerned, the forward-deployed troops would immediately be involved, which would in turn guarantee that the US, with all its military might, would assist. A second function of such forces, if the local forces were not strong enough, was to gain time for the US to deploy more forces into the theatre, to bring US strength up to the full number required for combat.

As explained earlier, the US maintains significant forward-deployed forces in the Western Pacific, in Japan, South Korea and in the US territory of Guam. Because the Western Pacific is mostly ocean, the US has more navy and air forces in this theatre and fewer army forces (the US Marines in Japan being part of the US Navy). A notable feature of Western Pacific theatre deployments is that the US does not maintain any forces on the island of Taiwan, even though this is usually seen as the most likely focus of an attack by China. This is because the US has long believed that in a conflict with China, the US could control the Taiwan Strait, between the Chinese mainland and Taiwan, with navy and air forces alone. (These forces were sometimes referred to as 'blocking forces' because they would block a Chinese invasion fleet.) What changed this belief was the development of Chinese military capabilities.

In its 2018 report, the bipartisan National Defense Strategy Commission (a Congressional body that makes suggestions as to what might be in both the National Security Strategy and its subordinate National Defense Strategy) expressed concern that 'China's missile, air, surface, and undersea capabilities' would grow and potentially make it too costly for the US to respond to Chinese military aggression in the Taiwan Strait. Since 2018, the Chinese military has only improved the capacity and range of these capabilities, especially within the Taiwan Strait.

If the US is not able to stop a Chinese attack on Taiwan via blocking forces in the Taiwan Strait, then it has only a limited number of other options. It would have to switch to relying on US and allied aircraft based in South Korea, Japan and Guam; to utilising one or two nuclear submarines that are almost permanently present in the vicinity of Taiwan, and others that could be called upon quickly to attack an invading force; and, possibly, increasing the number of US surface fleets that could approach Taiwan from the second island chain. These measures, perhaps backed by long-range bombers based in more distant places such as Diego Garcia in the Indian Ocean, provide only limited confidence that China could still be deterred.

The 2018 Report advocated steps:

> to strengthen the reach, agility, and survivability
> of American and partner blocking forces already
> forward positioned in and around the first island
> chain. By raising the costs and increasing the
> uncertainty of success for Beijing, a more robust
> posture would be more likely to deter aggression.
> Ready and capable blocking forces can also provide
> valuable time for surge forces to arrive from outside
> the region.[11]

In summary, because of the strength of the People's Liberation Army (PLA) in the Taiwan region and its ability to dominate this region and interfere with the deployment of US forces from outside the Western Pacific, the Commission recommended in 2018 that US forces be permanently located within the region so they don't have to expose their vulnerabilities in moving there during a period of tension or actual conflict. Such a move would be a significant change in policy by the US and its allies and would be seen by China as an aggressive move; indeed, China has said that forward deploying US troops to Taiwan would be considered an act of war. The commission went on to stress:

> Defeating an attempted fait accompli attack (surprise attack) by Beijing will not be easy. Once hostilities commence, US surge forces trying to get to the region can reasonably expect to be inundated with a range of attacks before they arrive and likely even before they depart the United States. Airlift and air-refuelling challenges will impair any effort to get assets to the region quickly. That puts a premium on strengthening US and partners' military capability pre-positioned along the first island chain. The next National Defense Strategy, therefore, should prioritise this effort and support projects and activities such as those promoted by Congress'[s] Pacific Deterrence Initiative.[12]

What the National Defense Strategy Commission is advocating as a feature of the next US National Defense Strategy is a 'strengthened forward defence posture', that is the permanent location of a much larger number of US and allied troops, ships and aircraft permanently deployed either on Taiwan or in the islands around Taiwan, referred to here as the first island chain. This is intended to overcome the problems that would be faced if China conducted a surprise attack and if China had the ability to reach out and interfere with the deployment of US forces from more distant bases. Such a recommendation is only valid as long as those forward-deployed forces are not themselves subject to the surprise attack referred to. Many of the US bases in the first island chain are now well within range of Chinese missiles and rockets, and so are vulnerable.

The Pacific Deterrence Initiative mentioned in the above quote is not a new idea, and is based on the 2014 European Deterrence Initiative, stemming from the perceived weakness of the US military in Europe and its inability to deter Russia's annexation of Crimea in 2014. Members of Congress specifically asked the Commander of the US Indo-Pacific Command, Admiral Phil Davidson, to submit a costed list of capabilities that would be necessary to deter Chinese military action in the region for which he was responsible. What they received in early 2020 was a US$20 billion wish list for the next six years. It envisaged a $1.6 billion defensive ring around Guam, millions for partner nations, and increased stockpiles of long-range weapons. Davidson called his plan 'Regain the Advantage', which indicates how the key US commander in Australia's region sees his position: he has lost the advantage.

Congressional commentary supporting Davidson's plan reflected 'bipartisan frustration with the Pentagon', which, it was claimed, continued to fall short of providing answers. One senator noted: 'The National Defense Strategy is more than just about how many planes, ships and tanks we buy. It's also about making sure our forces can be in the right place, at the right time, with the right stuff.'[13]

The issue that is emerging in the Indo-Pacific is that the US is deficient in both the weapons of war and the operational concepts of how to use them. Australia's major ally cannot afford to be deficient in both forces and fighting concepts, but Australia can hardly criticise, because (as I shall reveal in the next chapter) *our* deficiencies are even greater.

The question is: can any operational concept for the use of military forces that will not come fully into being for another six years deter China, especially if it is based on a bluff concerning its overall weak forces? And even if the US does send more permanent troops to bases in Japan, South Korea, Guam, Diego Garcia or even Australia, it must also ensure the bases that host those forces are hardened and defended. This means that fuel storage, maintenance facilities for ships and aircraft, and headquarters are dispersed and duplicated in places where they can be attacked by rockets, missiles or aircraft; that aircraft and ships are not lined up in the open, inviting attack; and that all such bases are ringed by anti-aircraft and anti-missile defences. Few of these bases are currently hardened or defended, and to send more forces to vulnerable bases is no better than the US deploying its battleships from US west-coast bases and lining them up for the Japanese to attack at Pearl Harbor in 1941.

For military power to deter, it must be real. Before any serious rethinking of Beijing's current policies of repression at home and aggressive competition abroad, China's leaders would need to be deterred by real evidence that the US is more resilient than they thought, and that the US could win a military confrontation. The Chinese leadership must be convinced, and they are smart enough to see through any bluff or bluster.

* * *

The most basic objective of the democratic nations of the world should surely be to avoid war with China if at all possible. This objective could of course be achieved by allowing China to incorporate Taiwan, even if it did it by force: a modern form of the policy of appeasement. War would certainly be avoided, but at the cost of the freedom of 23 million Taiwanese and encouraging China to use intimidation to achieve other goals. Dealing with the issue of an illegally aggressive China in our region could then be put off, at least until China wanted to use force in some other illegal way.

Yet the rhetoric would suggest that the aim of the US and its allies is to secure Taiwan against illegal coercion, aggression and invasion, as they did in post–World War II Europe through the Cold War (1948 to 1991) and in various Asian countries, such as Malaya, where they opposed a communist takeover during the Malayan Emergency (late 1940s till the early 1960s); South Korea, where they fought in the Korean War in the 1950s; and Vietnam, where they unsuccessfully attempted to help South Vietnam fight off North Vietnam in the 1960s and 70s.

If the aim is to secure Taiwan against a Chinese takeover, there may be a number of ways of doing it. First, the Taiwanese should be assisted in every way to defend their own nation, which has been happening to some extent for decades now through Taiwan's purchase of advanced US weaponry, authorised under the US *Taiwan Relations Act* of 1979. In relation to this, questions have been asked in the US Congress about whether Taiwan is doing enough itself. These are legitimate questions if there is an expectation that friends across the world will come to help the Taiwanese in the event of an attack.

Taiwan's ground forces need to reform. This started early in 2021 with the imposition of a new army structure more suited to wartime, in which operations are decentralised

A column of Taiwanese armoured vehicles on the move during a military exercise simulating a Chinese invasion of Taiwan, in November 2021. *(Getty)*

through regional commanders. A submarine production facility was opened that will manufacture eight new diesel-electric attack submarines, with assistance from the US, and in September 2021 the Taiwanese launched a new warship with air-defence capabilities and anti-ship missiles. Taiwan also plans to spend $1.4 billion on more fighter jets (F-16s) and more air-defence missiles to counter China's fighters.

These are admirable improvements, but it may all be too little, too late. Taiwan's military budget for 2022–23 is US$16.9 billion, only a small increase on this year's US$16.2 billion, whereas China has said it will raise its defence spending next year by 6.8%, still impressive but a little less than its long-term average of 8% a year. Taiwan has stated that it will commit an additional US$9 billion to its military over the next five years. But five years is a long time. It is certainly on the edge of many predictions of a likely invasion timeline, including mine, and longer even than the predictions of Taiwan's defence minister, who has an interest in portraying the shortest threat period possible.

Due to the confidence that a US fleet in the Taiwan Strait would physically block such an attack, for decades no one really worried about Taiwan's ability to defend itself from invasion. The Taiwanese became complacent because the US Navy carried the burden. Nowadays Taiwan has plans to buy long-range cruise missiles that could be used against an invasion fleet while it is on the water or just after it lands, but the improvement of China's amphibious capability means that China could still land despite these missiles, so the deficiencies in Taiwan's army must be further improved. Taiwan has a small fleet of US F-16 fighters, which are too few to stop the Chinese air force's jets dominating the island. As noted above, it plans to buy more, but even if the number of fighters was doubled, Taiwan could field only half the number with which China would likely attack. Simply put, Taiwan is nowhere near where it needs to be.

Of particular interest, and reflecting the sympathy that Taiwan has within the US Congress, Senator Josh Hawley, a member of the US Senate Armed Services Committee, recently introduced an *Arm Taiwan Act* which, if passed, would 'ensure Taiwan has the ... defenses it needs to deter a Chinese invasion'.[14]

The big issue is that Taiwan's defence spending is only 2.1% of its GDP, an amount far too small to counter China's military and not proportional for a very prosperous nation. The proposed *Arm Taiwan Act* requires that Taiwan spend at least 3% of its GDP on defence, ensuring that it plays its part if its allies are prepared to play their part. The Act quite logically focuses on Taiwan's reserve personnel. Taiwan has a population of 23 million and a claimed reserve of nearly 2.2 million soldiers, but US assessment of the military reserve force is that it is both declining and woefully underprepared. To ensure that Taiwan's reservists are effective and ready, the bill demands that its equipment be modernised and a review of how this reserve force will fight if an invasion occurs, so the reservists can better operate with active forces and with allies.

The *Arm Taiwan Act* favours weapons such as land-based anti-ship missiles (referred to as asymmetric defences because supposedly for a smaller outlay they give a greater return) over expensive submarines that would take years to develop, or fighter jets that would be inferior to China's. It proposes that the US match Taiwan's improvement in its military resolve with what is called the Taiwan Security Assistance Initiative. This would provide US$3 billion from US coffers each year from 2023 to 2027 to the US

Department of Defense for equipment, training and other support to build US capability to assist Taiwan.

In a stinging but constructive opinion piece in *Newsweek*, defence expert Sam Abodo concluded: 'From reserve numbers to fighter jets, Taiwan is playing catch-up in a military build-up race it will never win ... Senator Hawley gets Taiwan right: The *Arm Taiwan Act* solidifies the United States' commitment to its democratic partner, reorients its defense to more reasonable priorities and conditions assistance on matching investments. For these reasons, Congress must waste no time passing it.'[15] The bill was introduced in January 2022, referred to the Committee on Foreign Affairs and, at the time of writing, has not been passed.

A second way to secure Taiwan and deter China from military action would be, as discussed previously, for a relatively small number of foreign troops to be deployed to Taiwan to act as a tripwire force, which would, in certain circumstances, guarantee the subsequent arrival of US reinforcements. The current US policy of having no troops at the likely point of action on Taiwan is one of ambiguity and does not compel the US to become militarily engaged should Taiwan be attacked.

A third way of guaranteeing Taiwan's security – again assuming there is a change to the US policy of ambiguity – would be to locate a significant number of foreign forces, doubtless mainly American, on the 'front line' beside

Taiwanese forces, to form an integrated part of the defence of Taiwan. As previously discussed, this was the strategy that guaranteed European security for decades against the Warsaw Pact. Even with US and other troops permanently located on the inner German border, the US regularly practised the movement of even more troops from the US to Germany as reinforcement. Even Russia did not have the ability to prevent such massive sea and air movement at the time.

A fourth method of deterring Chinese aggression, according to thinking at the time when battles in the Taiwan Strait were envisaged, would be to use a small number of the most highly capable weapons systems, such as nuclear-powered attack submarines lurking somewhere close to Taiwan, which if the Chinese mounted a D-Day-style invasion, could interfere with or even deter the maritime component of a Chinese invasion. China of course would know that the submarines were in the region because the US admits to them being there and so would have to take them into account in their battle plans. In addition, US air power mounted from regional bases in South Korea, Japan and Guam, and more distant bases such as Diego Garcia or Australia, or from US Navy carrier battle groups at sea, could be used to support Taiwan without being located *on* Taiwan. China's reaction to these strategies, and how it might negate them, will be discussed later.

All of these strategies are relevant to the Taiwan scenario only if that scenario involves a Chinese fleet being assembled in mainland seaports and airports then moving across the Taiwan Strait, protected by China's warships and aircraft, and carrying out a sea and air landing. This would then be opposed by Taiwanese forces and by US air and sea power based out of regional bases and aircraft carriers that were not themselves subject to attack. As Chinese military capability increases, however, as we have seen, other options are becoming available to China, most notably removing the US from the Western Pacific and *then* 'reincorporating' Taiwan into the PRC. So, unless the US and its allies begin to think much more broadly and start looking at other options available to them, we might all be preparing for the wrong war.

All of this complicates the Taiwan issue from Australia's perspective, and it becomes legitimate for Australians to ask: if the US is ambiguous as to whether it will assist Taiwan and its 23 million citizens in the event of a Chinese invasion, might it feel the same way about 25 million Australians?

CHAPTER 7

THE RESPONSE: AUSTRALIA

There is change in the wind for Australians. After 75 years of one of the most secure existences in human history, most Australians have either become deeply complacent about issues of national security or have never even considered them. Those attitudes are changing, along with government policy, but not fast enough and not comprehensively enough.

In the recent past, there seemed to be a high degree of confidence that national security was something the government could manage. The government would tell the people when they should begin to worry. But in the face of a highly aggressive China, and with the real possibility of war now looming, many Australians have *already* begun to worry.

Australia is a prosperous nation, yet a deeply insecure one. This is a situation that has developed over many decades, and at the hands of many governments. Over the entire post–World War II period, Australia has been mainly a strategy-*taker*, not a strategy-*maker*. We have had the luxury of this contrariness because we have been allied with the US,[1] whose world role over those 75 years has been to provide security and prosperity to many countries, not just Australia.

As a result, we have prioritised prosperity over security. We have been remarkably successful as regards everything *except* our national security. It has been an easy ride along with the US and we have produced an extraordinary nation, if a complacent one. We have been very happy to live with whatever the US strategy of the day was, while having very little input, if any. As a substitute for strategy, we have expressed ourselves as having interests and values and, in some ways, tried to act accordingly.

Our dues to the US for 75 years of security have been paid by military involvement in many conflicts at America's side, leading to our identification as a close US ally. But all of those conflicts have been distant from our shores and have not involved critical, existential issues for Australia. We who fought in them classified them as 'wars of choice' because Australia could choose whether to participate, choose what forces we sent, choose when we sent those forces, choose what they did when they arrived in the operational area, and choose when we brought those forces home. At no stage did Australia have to commit to actually win. At no stage did we have to seriously pay heed to what the enemy would do, because we had so much choice, and when things were not going well, or when the US had decided it had had enough, we brought our forces home. Because we had these options, Australia did not need to have a military with high levels of readiness to go to war (which is expensive) nor did we need the most up-to-date equipment or even a wide range of forces, because what we did not have, the US had and so could support us logistically or on the battlefield.

Compared with the strategic environment that Australia faces now, where a major power could dominate the region at very short notice and where our major ally may not be able to provide the assistance we always took for granted, past wars of choice were easy. In those wars, failure was impossible above the tactical level because we did not decide which operations were to be conducted or how success was to be defined. In some of those wars, the size of our military contingent or how ready they were to fight did not even matter because the presence of the Australian flag beside the US and other countries' flags gave legitimacy to US claims of wide support. What was of importance to Australia was to be regarded by the US as an important ally, so that if in the future Australia needed US help in a more serious war, there was a greater chance of Australia receiving it.

Preparation and participation in a comfortable, distant and cheap war of choice is far easier than one in which

Australian forces must commit to being prepared to win. Because of the importance of commitment to winning possible wars, and not just participating, those of us in the military who were keenly aware of the deficiencies in our defence forces, called these new forms of warfare 'wars of commitment'. Behind this view, held widely in the thinking parts of the ADF (Australian Defence Force), lay a deep knowledge of both the strengths and the weaknesses of Australia's defence force, especially if it had to be used without as much US support as we were used to, and against an adversary more demanding than the East Timor militia, the insurgents in Iraq or the Taliban in Afghanistan. Having fought those wars, we could see the problems Australia could have if we had to actually win.

Australia has performed very well at the lowest tactical level in the wars in which we have fought because our soldiers are well trained and generally well equipped for tactical warfighting, and we were never rushed in deploying forces because of the presence of the US or other allies, already in place. In all our wars and operational deployments except East Timor – and East Timor was a UN-endorsed stabilisation operation in which there was very little combat – we have fought within a warfighting and logistics system provided by allies, mainly the US. In wars of choice, Australia has not needed to supply the more difficult parts of full combat support, such as heavy artillery, helicopters and attack aircraft, or a complete logistical system with mass sea, air or protected road transport, large-scale storage facilities or even the full range of ammunition. We merely plugged into an ally's system.

Winning a war consists of achieving the war aims. Each war is different, but what is consistent in wars of commitment is that the enemy has a far greater say than in our wars of choice. Because of that, Australia must be able to design and conduct military operations to achieve a strategy by ourselves, even if it is within a coalition of some kind. This is far more difficult than it sounds, unless there is experience of conducting military campaigns and aligning them with political needs. And it is my contention that Australia is incapable of conducting and supporting such a coherent regional campaign of its own – a war of commitment – or, at present, fighting at all except as a small part of a strong US force. This reflects appallingly on our sovereignty as a nation and our view of national security.

In the early 2000s, Professor Paul Dibb, director of the Strategic and Defence Studies Centre, made a damning forecast about the nature of the defence force Australia was in the process of creating: 'If we are not careful [we] will produce a one-shot ADF with nothing left over after we have protected such a small and vulnerable force.'[2]

The results are clear to see today. The ADF, a force I grew up in and that I love and support, lacks lethality (its weapons are not powerful enough), sustainability (it cannot fight for long enough) and mass (it is not big enough). As the professor predicted, it is a 'one-shot' defence force, appropriate for the wars of the last 75 years but almost impotent for the coming decade.

Most Australians think that Australia's experience of war over the last 100-plus years is epitomised by the ANZAC spirit, and the view that despite failures we always win in the end. I don't agree. I have long believed that our experience of war as a nation has been one of unpreparedness for each and every war we have participated in, and that still holds today. It was massive failure after massive failure that created the need for the ANZACs to suffer, and it is to their everlasting credit that they overcame these disadvantages.

The greatest failure of any government is to not make reasonable preparations for the defence of the nation, and Australia has had a series of governments of all political persuasions who have failed in this respect. It is a moral failure of the highest order to expect that the spirit and blood of the nation will act as a substitute for proper preparations to face evil in this world.

In industrial-age warfare, such as World Wars I and II, it was possible to be unprepared and, with a bit of luck, to survive. In the 1920s and 30s, it was possible for Australia to have a minuscule regular army backed up by a larger militia, a small navy as an adjunct to the Royal Navy, and a 'weekend' air force. In those days a nation could mobilise itself relatively quickly and could lose battle after battle but still put the nation on a war footing and prepare and equip armies. Australia had created sizeable war industries and developed the fourth-largest air force in the world by the end of World War II, and an army so big that at a certain stage of the war parts had to be disbanded to make workers available for growing food. Australians could fight and fail, but learn and win.

The wars we face today are overshadowed by nuclear weapons, and although conventional weapons are still predominantly industrial-age, using chemical energy to create kinetic impact or blast on soft human bodies, they are enhanced by information-age technology. Today computer digits can propel bullets and warheads accurately towards targets. The next information-age war will probably occur with unprecedented violence and speed, and it is unlikely, if not impossible, that Australia will be able to conduct even modern mobilisation as it was able to do the last time the existence of this nation was at risk, in World War II.

Luck is important in all wars. In World War II it was luck and bravery – as well as preparation by the US – that allowed us to survive in the naval battles of the Bismarck Sea, the Coral Sea and Midway, and the land, sea and air battles of Milne Bay, Guadalcanal and Papua. We all need luck, but when we over-rely on luck or on hope, we go a long way towards demanding that a new generation of ANZACs suffer. The more we prepare, the less luck we need to have.

Australian governments were told time and time again during the 1920s and 30s that the next war would be against Japan. Imperial war plans envisaged the deployment of significant elements of the Royal Navy to the Far East to defend its Singapore base, which was to be strengthened and garrisoned as the pivot of the defence of Australia, New Zealand and Britain's Far East colonies. However, it was always clear that if the German navy was active in the North Sea, the Royal Navy might be unable to send a naval force to Singapore. Yet with full knowledge of this, Australia was willing to send its under-equipped and under-trained army to North Africa, its navy to the Mediterranean, and its young men to North America to be trained as air crew then sent to Europe or the Middle East, even though the German navy was indeed active in the North Sea.

What caused the dislocation in our strategic thinking that led us to ignore information that was provided to us time and again over two decades? Australian decision-makers knew that Japan could attack at any time, and that we could be on our own. Why was it that the Australian government of the day, still bearing the scars of World War I from just 20 years earlier, was willing to dispatch the only forces we had to the other side of the world? Then, having done this, based on a strategy of hope that the Japanese would not attack our region – and if they did the Royal Navy would save us – we put ourselves to the task of creating a new generation of ANZACs to fight against an enemy we considered, in our bigoted ignorance, to be an inferior race.

For the last 75 years, Australian governments have been able to maintain defence spending at very low levels, affecting the purchase of new equipment and enabling only minimal training. My father, who was a soldier in World War II, would probably have recognised the structure and equipment of the infantry battalion that I commanded 40 years later.

It was embarrassing to be part of a nation that built warships after the Russians invaded Afghanistan in 1980 that we proudly admitted were fitted for, but didn't have, weapons! The intention was that the weapons could be added at some future time, thereby saving money in the short term. It was embarrassing to be in the military of a nation that maintained our land force at such low numbers of personnel and levels of equipment-readiness that critical tactical commanders could not be trained except at the most basic tactical level because their instruction was always theoretical and never practical, and where units and equipment had to be rebuilt to be deployed even to minor conflicts post-Vietnam, as we had to do with armoured vehicles over several months before our troops could be deployed to Muthanna Province in Iraq in 2005.

Our air force in the 1960s and 70s had no balance between combat aircraft that did the fighting and critical support aircraft, such as refuelling, command and control, intelligence collecting, and transport aircraft. It held almost no stocks of ammunition or missiles, due to our inability to produce anything much above small-arms ammunition. Our ability to deploy air force fighting units outside their peacetime airfield was severely limited. We ignored (and continue to ignore) our lack of production and storage of liquid fuel for civilian as well as military needs, relying mainly on overseas production of crude oil or refined product (aviation fuel, petrol and diesel) and pretended that our lines of communication by sea and air, by which liquid fuel was brought to Australia, would always be open – the classic example of a strategy of hope. We assumed that anything we had been too blinkered to provide for ourselves could be purchased and transported to Australia across hostile oceans in times of tension or war, in ships that we did not own.

Despite some improvements, those strategic chickens have now come home to roost.

* * *

Although we have been at war many times since 1945, Australian society has hardly been affected. As I have said, this has led to the highest imaginable degree of complacency within the general population on the issue of national security. Although some views have changed in recent times, Australia lacks both resilience and self-reliance, where resilience means the ability to take a hit, such as the reduction or cessation of shipping due to international tensions or war, and self-reliance refers to the ability that this country has to domestically manufacture the goods and services that we need – not what we 'want' but what we need.

Australians have long been consoled by the fact that we are far from regional trouble spots. If war ever occurs, this theory goes, it will be fought by the ADF in some distant theatre and, just like before, will not affect the everyday lives of Australians.

Most Australians who bother to think about the possibility of a regional war with China probably believe that the ADF can defend us. After all, governments tend to talk up the ADF at every opportunity and seem to spend a lot of money on it. (This, in my observation, is also a view held by most federal politicians.) And, returning to the point I have made repeatedly, most Australians also think that US military power is infinite and that, regardless of what we do, our great friend will always come to our rescue. Yet, as I pointed out in the previous chapter, since the Cold War ended in 1991 this has not been a true depiction of US military power. Comparisons with US success in facing down Russia no longer apply. There is still an element of truth in our belief in a very powerful US, but it has now become a very dangerous view, encouraging complacency.

It is unreasonable to expect that today's Australians have the same attitude to and knowledge of war as the immediate post–World War II generation, because most of us have no relevant lived experience. Since 1945, the essence of what has passed for grand strategy in Australia has been to deter conflict by being allied to the US. This has made us one of the richest countries in the world, because we did not have to exorbitantly fund our own defence, nor did we have to secure the sea lanes along which our exports were carried. We have one of the highest standards of living in the world, we have the world's 13th largest GDP,[3] we are a liberal democracy, we are a member of two of the most influential economic and security world groups, the G20 (Group of Twenty) and the g7+, and we are in a number of treaty alliances with the US and other countries. With a population of 25.8 million, Australia occupies a continent rich in exportable natural resources at the strategically important intersection of the Indian and Pacific Oceans.[4] Yet as a country with a strong economy, good diplomacy and leadership (all part of national power), we are mind-numbingly weak in terms of hard (military) power.

Under the reassuring umbrella of US power, initially we traded over secure sea lines of communication, then in the information age we embraced globalisation, assuming we could purchase products at cheap prices from overseas industries forever, and so we exported much of our manufacturing base to countries that produced the items more cheaply. But, as we are now discovering, having passed through the COVID pandemic, our desire to buy everything cheaper from overseas and so to 'export' critical industries and even our shipping, has frightening implications for our national security. We have become over-reliant on one trading partner – China – and it is now a potential adversary that is using this dependence against us.

China's attitude towards Australia has deteriorated markedly since about 2016, but particularly after we had the gall to suggest in 2020 that an inquiry into the source of COVID should be conducted. Much of this hostility was expressed through CCP mouthpieces in the media, such as the *Global Times*, but the rhetoric indicates an attitude. Australia was certainly targeted by China in this manner earlier and more than most other countries, but our strong reaction to this bullying, and the backing we received from many other countries, has been an example to all. It is likely that our close relationship with the US, a relationship that has grown stronger as a result of China's bullying, was one of the reasons that China targeted Australia. But it has not worked as China intended and it did not flow on to the US through Australia. China has not brought Australia to our knees. But China's actions and our embrace of globalisation do have long-term implications for Australia in that our prosperity has been achieved at the expense of our security, making Australia vulnerable to the kind of coercion and bullying that is now a hallmark of the CCP under President Xi Jinping. And it makes us very weak if China's actions move into conflict.

We have long believed in the myth that everyone loves Australia, but many Australians' views of international relations are shaped by a very limited experience of the world, extending no further north than the holiday island of Bali. China's actions have come as a shock because we have not been the target of direct coercion by a large regional power since World War II. Polls indicate that Australians are adjusting to the CCP view that Australia represents everything China is not, and that therefore Australia should not seek to prosper from our relationship, or even have a close relationship with China.

From my own informal polls of friends and political colleagues, I have learned that most now share an awareness of the threat from China, and most know that, in the extreme, it may manifest itself as war resulting from Chinese moves against Taiwan. According to successive Lowy Institute polls, since 2017 Australians' trust and confidence in China and its leaders have noticeably declined. In 2021, 63% of Australians saw China as 'more of a security threat to Australia', a 22-point increase on 2020. In the same poll, 93% of Australians saw China's military activities in our region as having a negative influence on their views of China. On 4 October 2021, Newspoll claimed that 75% of those polled believed that China posed a significant threat to Australia's national security. Over the period of 23–27 February 2022, at the start of the Russian invasion of Ukraine, Newspoll ran a poll on both Russia and China, finding that 74% of Australians believed that China posed a threat and 64% of Australians believed that Russia posed a threat to Australians.

If Australia is to take that threat seriously and acknowledge the possibility of a war with China, it is essential for us to understand the probable nature of that war. The consequences of preparing for no war, or the wrong war, or even of overpreparing for an unlikely war, are either the disaster of losing when an adversary executes its war, or a massive waste of scarce resources. History is replete with examples of preparing for the wrong war or the wrong battle: Pearl Harbor and other allied bases in the Pacific in 1941, the German attack on France through the Ardennes and the Maginot line in 1940, the Chinese attack across the Yalu River in 1950, the German attack on Russia in 1941, the Iraqi attack on Kuwait in 1990, and the US invasion of Iraq in 2003 are just a few.

At present, the war Australia seems to be preparing for is one where China instigates a major amphibious and airborne attack across the Taiwan Strait while the attacking force is subject to US air and navy counterattacks. We seem to believe that there will be time for Australia to prepare a force of ships and aircraft capable of fighting a daunting adversary and dispatch them from Australia to assist a US force somewhere in the region, then support the US in whatever it decides to do. There is also an expectation that like all the wars that Australia has been involved in over the last 75 years, casualties in personnel and equipment will be (comparatively) light.

Given the lack of action by governments over many years, we erroneously believe that in such a war Australian society is unlikely to be impacted any more than it was by our previous post–World War II conflicts. There seems to be an implicit belief, too, that the US coalition of forces will win, and our forces deployed to that war will return victorious to Australia. But, as we have seen, a D-Day-style attack on Taiwan is only one option for China, and it could be disastrous if Australia is not prepared for other scenarios too.

It is essential for us to make a national commitment to winning and have significant forces that are highly ready at all times – solid forces that have the lethality modern war demands. These forces may need to fight over a long period of time and sustain significant losses – because war often involves learning through failure, with costs in lives and materiel – and will need to be substantial enough not just to fight one battle in one place, but to take part in campaigns consisting of a series of battles within an overall military strategy.

Even more importantly, the nation that backs up its defence force must be resilient and self-reliant. In the Westminster system this makes the policy, direction and coordination of national security the responsibility of the Prime Minister through Cabinet. Australians will need to feed and provide for themselves when cut off from outside support, and to establish an industrial base that can build and maintain military equipment, innovating to a world standard to support the military materiel that we have to purchase from overseas.

It is my judgment – military and otherwise – that Australia cannot do this at present and will need considerable time to develop the capability to do so. Unless we can dramatically change our ways, the question we will need to address as a nation is whether we can achieve much at all in the three-to-five-year predicted timeframe for a regional war. At present we cannot deter either a regional war or a collateral attack on Australia as part of that war, and we can do nothing to minimise the impact of such a collateral attack. This is a terrifying national weakness.

Of course, diplomacy is our first line of defence and our diplomats work very hard at this. We were in probably the most reliable alliance in the world, ANZUS – the Australia,

New Zealand, United States alliance, which was activated for the first time on the occasion of 9/11 by Prime Minister John Howard and then renewed in a different form in 2021 by Prime Minister Scott Morrison in the form of AUKUS, the agreement between Australia, the United Kingdom and the United States. But we do need to consider the fact that being in such a strong alliance with the US may have made us a target for bullying in the past from China and may in the future make us a target for attack if a war occurs.

National security requires a national approach, and, as I say often, it takes a nation to defend a nation. This in turn requires government to lead the way in every aspect of national life. If we cannot solve every national security

US President Joe Biden, flanked by Australian Prime Minister Scott Morrison and UK Prime Minister Boris Johnson, announces the formation of the new AUKUS trilateral security initiative, in September 2021. *(Alamy)*

deficiency at once, we need to decide on our priorities. But how can we ever decide on priorities unless a comprehensive scan of all likely threats, and what Australia needs for the necessary responses, is carried out?

There is no indication that this has occurred, even at the highest level of classification. If it had, the results would be observable at lower, unclassified levels. And if in fact there *is* a comprehensive national security strategy, what is the benefit of keeping its existence secret? The only alternative explanation is that there *is* no strategy, and this is reinforced by the patently inadequate state of national security in Australia.

A comprehensive process of national security that improves our defences and resilience is surely worth advertising. If we have serious national and military vulnerabilities, as I maintain, and if many in the government and the population are nourishing the belief that we have somehow reached national security perfection when we have not, then something is deeply wrong and should not be hidden.

Certainly, the last Coalition government began to display a healthy concern about our strategic environment, and many Australians are showing a change of attitude towards China. Yet a better knowledge of what a modern regional war might be like would give both government and people a much more realistic view of Australia's national security strengths or weaknesses.

In my parliamentary committee duties I have often asked defence officials what war they are preparing for, and I have never received an answer. Most retreat behind a 'classified' barrier. Either they do not know or are unprepared to commit themselves. Yet, by comparison, when I asked the Japanese military attaché the same question in a defence committee hearing, his answer was straightforward: war against China and Russia.

As I have discussed, war is more likely than most leaders admit, because of the movement in the Western Pacific of sizeable military forces in relative proximity to each other on a regular basis in disputed areas, as well as the often professed readiness of China to use force.[5] If war occurs suddenly, or if there is some unpredictable incident or even an accidental clash that does not get out of hand and is contained, Australia may or may not get involved immediately if the clash involves other nations' forces. Given the small size of Australia's military, its current low state of readiness and our distance from the likely combat areas, Australia may take longer to get to the fight than the time it takes for the fight (or at least the first stages of a war) to be resolved, especially if China is successful.

If we *are* somehow involved, we go to war as a highly vulnerable nation. Australians in general, but officials and leaders in particular, have little or no conception of how such a war might be conducted, or how to prepare for it. Those with a military background have little direct experience, because we have not seen a strategic situation like this for decades.

I would like to see the views expounded in this book being refined by the knowledge and opinions of others through constructive debate. But that debate is not occurring. Talking about something is the first step towards action, so let's at least start talking.

CHAPTER 8

CONCEPTS OF WAR

Modern military theory links a nation's overall strategy, the operational concepts required to achieve that strategy, and the tactics that make the operational concepts possible, all of which must be aligned to achieve success in war. This is a well-known idea, but very hard to do. A great aphorism, which is usually attributed to the famous Chinese general, military strategist and philosopher Sun Tzu, from around the fifth century BC, says: 'Strategy without tactics is the slowest route to victory. Tactics without strategy is noise before defeat.'[1] What this means is that it is more important in war to get your overall strategy right first and then over time you can develop the tactics to be victorious. If you try to do it the other way around, you can be as good as it is possible to be in low-level tactical fighting, and all you are doing is making noise before you are defeated.

For Sun Tzu, strategy sat directly above tactics, but as war became more complex, the need for an operational concept to link tactics and strategy evolved, particularly after World War II. For Australia in the twenty-first century, facing a strategic environment dominated by the threat from China, we must get all three right before the war begins, because modern war might provide very little time to fail, learn and improve. It might be all over too fast.

Strategy is about ends, ways and means in a very general sense. For a military force, it is critically important to know, to the maximum extent possible, how an operation or a campaign or a war is going to be conducted, and how, where and who the force will fight. Predicting this is a large part of the 'art' in *The Art of War*. It is about intuition, where intuition is about making judgments from a base of deep experience of a subject. And, finally, it is about the willingness to take risk, but calculated risk based on facts and judgment.

A successful strategy must not stifle initiative, but by defining boundaries and objectives you can *open up* initiative at every government level and focus a nation's efforts. Leaders who claim that strategy stifles initiative reveal their lack of experience with good strategy, and they are perhaps displaying a need to control everything centrally and personally, which very quickly becomes impossible. There are severe limits to a centralised approach, and I believe we are seeing those limits in Australia at present, where we are addressing elements of national security one by one – modern manufacturing, storage of liquid fuel, nuclear submarines, sovereign missile production, cyber warfare – without an overall strategy that indicates priorities, timing and where and when risks can be taken.

The need for strategy might be an esoteric point for some people, and those who advocate for strategy might be accused of mere process and pedantry, but strategy is just as important now as it was 2500 years ago. However, just having a national security strategy, as the US does, will not guarantee success. There is no point in developing a national strategy that the nation or the military cannot achieve at an operational or a tactical level. The strategy must be as appropriate as possible, it must apply not just to the defence force but across the nation, it must influence the actions of every government minister and every department without stifling them, and it must be executed in a way that holds us all accountable. Do we have enough industry with which to produce weapons and with which to innovate? Can we feed our people? Can we keep a secret? Can we provide the one thing that is still necessary for industry, agriculture and warfighting – liquid fuel? Can we mobilise the nation in a modern sense, to move the nation from a peacetime focus to one of war in a reasonable period? Are we resolved as a society to prosecute a war?

If you start with a good national security strategy – what you want to achieve overall across the nation and the ways and means of doing it – you can derive subordinate strategies (or what the strategy purist might prefer to call 'plans') for each area of government (generally in Australia's case corresponding to government ministries), and then you have started down the road to success. Even the process of deriving the strategy will almost immediately pay dividends. In the case of the military, as an example, a national defence strategy should be defined from the national security strategy, which is then refined into one or more operational concepts stating how a nation will fight, and then solutions like the number and type of weapons needed will be much more obvious and defendable, and so procurement priorities can be set.

A serious attempt must be made by government to get the strategy right to begin with, and hopefully a good strategy lasts, but if it needs to be changed, it must be changed. However, the operational concepts and the tactics employed must be infinitely variable in modern, fast-moving and decisive conflicts, and in the period leading up to a war as the situation changes.

Sadly, though, it is rare that a nation's strategy, operations and tactics are aligned at the start of a war. Normally they align the hard way, through the impetus of defeat, as we have seen in our long world wars, where there were opportunities to try, fail and improve. But in modern warfare, in the era of attacks in space and cyberspace and with missiles and rockets that are hyper-accurate over vast distances, defeat may be so devastating and quick in the first instance that, unlike in past wars, learning and recovery may not be possible. This is the risk that Australia and its allies are taking at this very moment.

A nation that does not first set out to get its strategy right, while putting significant energy into totally implausible tactics regarding how the nation will react and how the military will fight, risks defeat. Success will not come to a nation that cannot sustain its warfighting capability in the ways required to achieve the strategy it adopts. If it does not have the tactical equipment and the training for its military, if it lacks resolve as a nation or it cannot feed its people or make and maintain the tools of war, it is not in the game.

Since 1976, Australia has produced defence and foreign affairs white papers every few years to summarise our security situation. Labor prime minister Julia Gillard bears the distinction of having introduced Australia's first national security strategy, just months before Labor's electoral defeat in 2013, but it was too little too late, was not even debated by parliament and never had the chance to become institutionalised. Apart from that, we have never produced an overall national security strategy from which all other subordinate national strategies might be derived. We have never really needed to, because our great and powerful ally the US has always been there.

It is my opinion that the strategy stated or implied in every defence white paper since 1976 – a time when, as a serving soldier, I was a very interested customer of defence policy – has never been achievable by the ADF. That, I think, is a damning accusation.

Because we do not have a comprehensive national security or defence strategy, it is very hard to test, say, any proposed equipment purchases against an operational concept, much less something as vague as the resilience or resolve of the nation.

For years we pretended to have a 'Defence of Australia' strategy, which was designed in 1987 by the Hawke Labor government to justify cutting defence expenditure. The intelligence community and bureaucracy fell into line. Every experienced person exposed to the Defence of Australia strategy knew that it could only be achieved by the small, impotent military we were permitted to have if our enemy was as weak as it was in the exercises we conducted.

Our navy and air force just ignored the strategic guidance over this period and kept doing what they could do with the funds they had. But the army, sadly, not only listened to it but, like good armies everywhere, started to believe it, with the consequences that it reduced it from a good conventional army that had fought well in several vastly different wars (Korea, Malaya and Vietnam) to what was essentially a police field or paramilitary force. We then equipped the army with weapons and vehicles totally unsuited to modern war. Our strategy and our tactics were seriously misaligned, and a generation of military leaders and military nous was lost, until we were forced by East Timor, Iraq and Afghanistan to think, equip and train for a more modern form of warfare. It was only recently, under the last Coalition government, that we started to bring the three services into the twenty-first century, but at its current pace it will take a very long time, time we may not have.

Average but narrow policy, with no real-world outcomes or accountability, has put Australia at great risk. The endpoint of national security policy, despite what many bureaucrats believe, should never be just policy itself, but should be a secure and strong sovereign nation. And Australia is weak. For so many years now, the leaders of our nation, and the bureaucrats in and out of uniform, have often been more interested in producing paper policy than examining whether the nation's diplomats or soldiers could actually achieve the policy in question.

The danger of this disconnect between policy and reality is now being seen, because an existential threat to this country has appeared in the form of an aggressive China. But still Australian 'strategists', in and out of government, revel in clever words spoken and written in their alternative reality and attend to the national security of this nation with glacial slowness, as though today's China did not exist and there were no possible threats for the next 10 or 20 years.

If there had been a culture of comprehensive strategy-making within Australian government over the last few decades, via some kind of national security mechanism or council, I wonder whether someone might have spoken out about the caution that needs to be exercised if the market is left to decide what industries we give up on in Australia and send overseas? But those concerns were never raised and now, when we need industries and shipping and other strategically important national capabilities, we are left in the invidious position of trying to recreate them. We are reaping the consequences of decades of decision-making failure.

Much of the commentary at the moment in Australia is totally captive to an out-of-date and dangerous view that no more money needs to be spent on defence and, instead, Australia should sacrifice one area of defence, decreasing the current level of expenditure on land warfare, for instance, to subsidise maritime, air, space or cyber warfare. Such thinking belongs to the Australia of the last 75 years, a time when we could choose when to participate in a war, and only send the forces we had and were prepared to deploy. The current force is not a force that we can commit to a serious war we have to win.

I do not question the motives of recent governments, but in the national security area we are a product of our strategic upbringing. For most of the last 75 years, Australia and its governments have expressed what they did primarily in terms of 'inputs' to security, not in terms of the 'outputs' that a nation needs. For most of the last 75 years, we judged ourselves by whether we had met a certain percentage of gross domestic product (GDP). The figure we settled on was 2%, though it has dropped below that. This figure was derived from the demands made by the US to its NATO partners, who were free-riding on the US by making a lesser contribution to European defence because the US was prepared to make such a large contribution.

Two per cent of GDP might have been the right amount to spend on defence for NATO countries while the US, paying up to 6% of GDP at times, was the most dominant power in the world. But now the question needs to be asked by all Australians: even if 2% was the right amount in the past, is it the right amount for Australia to pay for defence *now*, at a time when China, Russia, Iran and North Korea are rising to challenge the US, and US military power is declining?

When in government, we in the Coalition boasted that we had finally returned defence expenditure to 2% of GDP, after attacking our opponents for having allowed it to drop in 2013 to about 1.6%. Our Prime Minister and Minister for Defence then began saying that, if anything, 2% was a floor for spending. My view is that 2% has become not just irrelevant but dangerous.

Referring to our national security credentials in terms of defence spending might have been acceptable for most of the last 75 years, when the amount of money spent on defence was mostly decided by what was left over after everything else in the budget had been allocated. But today the dominant question for national security should not be how much do we spend on defence, but what war or wars are we preparing to win and what would that cost?

Money itself does not throw back the enemy from the gates or defeat the danger on our doorstep. In our strategic environment it only matters what we *do* with that money. Will 2% of GDP allow us to build sufficient modern ships to assist our allies in deterring conflict in the Western Pacific, and at the same time provide missile defence to vulnerable points on the Australian continent? Will 2% allow us to provide enough airborne fuel tankers to support our full range of fighter planes? Will there be enough liquid fuel at allied bases to supply these air tankers? Will we have enough missiles to support a modern war any time short of 10 or 20 years from now? If not, then something is desperately wrong with how we are thinking about defence.

The measure of what this nation does in terms of defence and national security is whether it meets the need. And my intention in this book is to define the need that must be met. At present, in the absence of a clear defence strategy, Australia has 'strategic objectives', as expressed in the 2020 Strategic Update of 'Shape, Deter, Respond', to guide defence planning, though sadly not national planning. The idea is to *shape* Australia's military strategic environment prior to conflict or war, to *deter* actions against Australia's interests, and to *respond* with credible military force when required.

Using Shape, Deter, Respond is admittedly slightly better than referring to our defence achievements in input terms – that is, the now meaningless 2% of GDP. At least Shape, Deter, Respond comes close to being an operational concept for an unstated war against an unstated enemy at an unstated time using unstated operational concepts and tactics. The problem is that there is a deep reluctance in government and the bureaucracy to go from these three well-intentioned words to stark reality, to add detail that lays out what is going to be shaped, what is going to be deterred and what will be responded to. Such words remain just words without appropriate critical detail. Without any detail, how can anyone – defence planners or the general public or even our potential adversaries – determine whether we have allocated enough resources to these three objectives, or whether we are deficient in any of them (and I believe we are deficient in at least two – Deter and Respond), and by which point we are supposed to have achieved them?

The essence of Australia's strategy must indeed be to *deter* war, but if we base that strategy on a bluff, then we can only bluff for so long, and China is not buying it. It must be assumed that China knows more about our national security, and particularly our defence potential, than 99.9% of Australians. In fact, China has called us out on our defence weakness, and laughs at us through the *Global Times*.

Deterrence is only successful if a nation can convince an adversary that in the event of war they will incur debilitating costs, and the adversary refrains from action. For the US, what must be deterred is relatively obvious: war with China. But Australia must be very careful about what we are trying to deter or we will look ridiculous. We cannot deter a war between China and the US; we are too small and weak. We can contribute to regional deterrence by committing our armed forces to a US-led coalition, but we have so few forces in our one-shot defence force that if we lose them – which we must accept as a genuine risk – we are in deep trouble.

If we are clever and lucky and we have enough time, we might be able to achieve alignment of Australia's national and defence strategies with how we fight the next war. But, of course, the whole process must start with a strategy, and any other approach is likely to be guided by the worst form of strategy: a strategy of hope.

* * *

Those outside the intelligence and policy communities often lack accurate information about important matters like military and civilian security. So we also need to ask ourselves: should we be talking about these matters at all? Some have criticised me for doing so, and claim I am exposing vulnerabilities.

My intention in this book is indeed to expose vulnerabilities, none of which is classified. I have been running the argument that Australia is inadequately defended since at least 2008, when my first book, *Running the War in Iraq*, was published.[2] But, really, I have held these views for the second half of my 40-year military career, which ended the same year – in 2008.

The main motivation behind my decision to originally offer myself for preselection as a Liberal Party senator for New South Wales was to address the issue of national security by joining the government with the best record on defence achievement, the centre-right federal Coalition government. I stated this clearly during each of my four Liberal Party preselections, when I offered myself to the party faithful to be chosen as a candidate. National security was a central theme in my first speech in the Senate.

On any number of occasions, I have confronted ministers and government officials and I have even been (very generously) given the privilege of addressing the National Security Committee of Cabinet on these issues. At no stage was I able to convince my colleagues of the merit of my argument, I think because the concept of war for Australians is so unfamiliar. In my last interaction, when I pointed out the need for a national security strategy, I was asked if having a national security strategy was likely to make the bureaucracy in Defence move faster than their current glacial pace – a 10- or 20-year time period to change major capabilities, as the progress of most of our major policies (infrastructure, submarines, missiles, cyber, etc.) illustrates. I answered that a strategy would not necessarily make things happen faster but that the right strategy might make the right things happen, which is better than rushing to failure by building the wrong capabilities for the wrong war, in a period that produces irrelevant results after we have lost the next war.

CHAPTER 9

CURRENT POLICY

Many Australians across this nation are uncomfortable with what Australia is doing in defence and national security, but, understandably, few if any have the experience to make a detailed judgment. Instead, they depend on me and others who are similarly qualified to provide what they are not getting from the government. What they *do* want is for the government to act, and to act effectively. Many are just not sure what 'effective' looks like.

Governments in Australia frequently say that they have no greater duty than to keep our people safe and protect our way of life for future generations. As a member of the recent Coalition government, I was impressed by the way prime ministers Tony Abbott, Malcolm Turnbull and Scott Morrison each improved upon their predecessors' approach to defence. Australia under the Coalition showed distinct signs of resolve. More money was allocated to defence and there was a plan as to how that money should be spent. In the past, the Coalition had reflected the complacent view of the Australian people towards defence in some ways, but more recently it led the Australian people much more effectively in this area. It does not reflect a partisan position to say that only the Coalition can be trusted on defence; this is what the record, at least of defence expenditure and projects started or completed, shows. But we will have to see how the new Labor government responds.

The aberration of Gillard's security strategy aside, Labor during the Rudd–Gillard–Rudd governments generally used defence as a cash cow to pay for its social programs, reducing the expenditure on defence to pre–World War II levels, 1.6% of GDP. This has meant that many of the programs that should be in place now, when Australia is facing an identifiable threat, are not there. The prime example is shipbuilding: the Labor Party did not lay down one keel during the entire time it was in power. As of May 2022, the Coalition had completed or started the building or purchase of 70 ships for the Royal Australian Navy.

The Australian political party known as the Greens has an ill-considered defence policy, essentially aimed at disarming Australia at a time when the region is more uncertain than it has been since 1945. If the new Labor government needs to rely on the Greens in government, then a suboptimal approach to defence might be the price it is prepared to pay.

Because we must prepare for the kind of war that I have described in this book, I believe Australia needs the Coalition. The last Coalition government did more for defence than any previous government since the end of the Vietnam War. But far, far more needs to be done, and I fear that only the Coalition has the attitude and knowledge to do this. Yet Australia now relies on a Labor government that will need to prove its credentials with regard to national security.

One of the real strengths of the Coalition is that backbench senators and members of parliament are permitted, in fact encouraged, to speak their minds. If they have experience and expertise in a particular area, they are given a hearing and listened to. Within the Coalition I have been given a hearing and listened to. I have made my points strongly and without prejudice. As I have said publicly, the biggest problem I faced as a member of the recent Coalition government was that because it had done so much for defence compared with previous governments, a request to do more could sound like whining. 'What more do you want us to do, Jim?' was not an unusual response to my suggestions.

The last Coalition government responded very well to the increase in the terror threat since 9/11, through often world-leading legislation, additional funding for security agencies, addressing cyber and online safety and restructuring government departments. It also responded very well by any international standard to the national security challenge of COVID-19 and its economic consequences. The enormous impact of COVID on our health and economic resilience was without doubt the most immediate national security threat for Australia in recent times, and could have remained so if the government's economic and health reaction had not been so effective. The Morrison government paid in excess of AUD$331 billion in COVID support payments to Australians during 2020 and 2021, payments that I fully supported, at a time when such an amount could have been used more directly to encourage self-reliance across the entire nation. I supported them because they were needed to keep workers in jobs and businesses running so that the economy could recover quickly, which it did. A healthy economy is the basis of national security.

The management of the pandemic left the Coalition government deeply experienced at governing during a crisis. Recovery from COVID is our most immediate challenge during 2022, but China's coercion and aggression in our region could lead to a far more dangerous crisis that the new Labor government will now need to manage.

* * *

On 1 July 2020, Prime Minister Scott Morrison gave a well-crafted and very tough speech to accompany a more formal strategic update of our defence policy. He also announced defence spending of AUD\$270 billion over 10 years – far, far too long a period. This new funding may *marginally* increase the ADF's lethality and sustainability once various types of missiles are procured and brought into service. Unfortunately, the investment will not increase the mass (size) of the ADF: \$270 billion is a very large amount of money, but it will not be enough to create a military, or a nation, that can face the emerging strategic environment with confidence.

Nevertheless, the speech itself was a good reaction to the aggression and coercion of China over the four years from 2016 to 2020. At the time, I totally supported the Prime Minister's approach, mainly because I had not heard anything like it for the 40 frustrating years that I had spent in the military. At the time of writing, just after the election of the new Labor government, it stands as our current defence policy, and so should be the subject of some discussion here.

Prime Minister Morrison spoke of 'Tensions over territorial claims rising across the Indo-Pacific region, as we have seen recently on the disputed border between India and China, and the South China Sea, and the East China Sea. The risk of miscalculation and even conflict is heightening.' As a result of this, he said, 'my government is making a further commitment to better position Defence to respond to rapid changes in the environment that I've noted'. He admitted: 'The ADF now needs stronger deterrence capabilities, that can hold potential adversaries, their forces and critical infrastructure at risk from a distance, thereby deterring an attack on Australia and helping to prevent war.'

The Prime Minister justified the approach and the extra resources by saying that 'The strategic environment and the heightened risk of miscalculation in the region [make] this a necessity. There's much more tension in the world these days. We need an ADF that is ready now, but is also future-ready.' This was an admission, I believe, that war is far more likely than most leaders are saying. I agree with the Prime Minister's assertion that war could occur at any time by mischance, but such an accidental conflict might at least be limited in some ways. A planned and intentionally executed war by China might not be limited in either time or space.

The Prime Minister, however, went on, saying that 'responding credibly to threats doesn't simply come down to the ADF. It's about the system that surrounds it, supports it – the ecosystem that it is a part of – and this is the hard bit, it's about the support and structures that [have] to do with the job.' This was the closest the Prime Minister came to asserting that it takes a nation to defend a nation.

Critically for this examination, the Prime Minister then said:

The strategic challenges of today and tomorrow call
Australia in many ways, as we've been called before

at difficult times ... 2020 has demonstrated once
again the multiple challenges and radical uncertainty
we face, eerily haunted by similar times many years
ago in the 1930s ... Our Defence Force will need
to be prepared for any future, no matter how
unlikely, and hopefully not needed in the worst of
circumstances.[1]

In this reference to the 1930s, which Prime Minister Morrison made in a number of other forums, he was most likely referring to the threats that appeared to peace in Europe and Asia during that period, and to the weak policy of appeasement adopted by European governments, which achieved nothing, was morally bankrupt as it divided up smaller nations across central Europe, and encouraged further intimidation, coercion and military action by Germany, Italy and Japan.

This was a very good speech by any measure. It would have been interesting to see how different a strategic update speech might have been only one year later, given that our relationship with China deteriorated even more in that period, and there were other developments, which I shall discuss below.

What the speech missed, though, except in a single obtuse reference – 'responding credibly to threats doesn't simply come down to the ADF' – was that, regardless of how well prepared the ADF might be, unless the Australian nation is also prepared for war, the ADF's efforts will come to not much at all. What the speech also lacked was a comprehensive view of national security, and a specific statement as to the nature of the war we are to prepare for, by when we must be prepared for it, and the changes needed in government to initiate those preparations. There was also no mention of the specific roles of each cabinet minister, because in our modern nation, every minister has national security responsibilities for which they should be held accountable through the National Security Committee of Cabinet.

In summary, there appears to be no coordinated national security strategy from any government that aims to produce an ADF that is lethal, sustainable and large enough in any timeframe. Neither does there appear to be a plan to produce a resilient and self-reliant Australia in anything like a reasonable period.

It is the job of governments to lead on national security issues. Much of the national security threat is seen as military, but the solution in Australia's case concerns the resilience and self-reliance of the whole nation. The Prime Minister's speech was aimed at the initiated, at the defence and thinktank communities and at policy wonks. But if the Australian people are to be carried along and support any government, then a clear and unclassified strategic assessment must at some stage be released to them. It is the people's security, and the people are paying for it. This is not something that governments or the intelligence community are likely to be comfortable with. But the Australian people deserve some straight talk about the security threats they face.

Regardless of what Australia decides to do, we need to begin with a comprehensive strategy. And most of that strategy should be made public.

* * *

The Coalition, however, had more important defence initiatives to come. On 16 September 2021, Prime Minister Morrison, along with the US President and the UK Prime Minister, announced the biggest development in Australian security since the 1950s. It was declared by the three leaders that an enhanced trilateral security partnership to be known as AUKUS (Australia, United Kingdom, United States) would be formed, and its first initiative would be Australia's acquisition of nuclear-powered submarine technology – the consequence, of course, being that Australia would no longer proceed with its existing French submarine program. Australia would also gain access to other US technologies (such as artificial intelligence and quantum computing), purchase missiles for current use, and be given assistance in developing a future missile manufacturing enterprise in South Australia.[2]

On 24 September, following the AUKUS announcement, Prime Minister Morrison joined the Minister for Foreign Affairs and the Minister for Defence in the US for the first ever in-person meeting of another significant grouping, the Quadrilateral Security Dialogue, known as the Quad, involving the US, Japan and India. There is no talk at this stage of a defence treaty between these nations. Although the Quad is not as attention-grabbing as AUKUS, it is probably as important, and the Quad meeting, attended in turn by former prime minister Morrison and recently by newly appointed Prime Minister Albanese, was an indication that China's aggressive attitude is coalescing the region, which is in Australia's interests.

Much of the significance of the better-known AUKUS agreement has been overshadowed by two issues: Australia's acquisition of nuclear submarines, and the fallout between Australia and France after the cancellation of the French submarine contract. There has been much criticism of the way our relationship with France, an important ally with common interests in our region, has been handled. In general, though, the announcement of the acquisition of nuclear submarines sometime in the future has been extraordinarily well received in Australia, indicating the unfocused concern Australians now have about their strategic environment.

The AUKUS agreement certainly caught Beijing's attention and resulted in a burst of hateful and threatening

CCP rhetoric, even though the AUKUS leaders never mentioned China directly. Ironically, AUKUS increases both the likelihood that China can be deterred from taking military action, and the likelihood that a war will occur sooner. The new alliance must make China consider the balance of power, both in the region and across the world. But it might also make the CCP think that if it wants to take Taiwan by force, it will have to act soon or it will not be able to act at all.

AUKUS came about as a result of the Coalition government's belief that our strategic environment had deteriorated to such a degree that we needed to reaffirm our relationship with the US in particular, but also with the UK, our traditional partner in security. It is not just *our* environment that is deteriorating, but that of the whole region, and we are not the only ones to see it. Other recent individual one-to-one agreements in our region, such as various agreements between the US and Japan, and South Korea and the Philippines, may also have the same contrary effect on China – that is, encourage an early decision by China to go to war.

In October 2021 – at the same time as it became public knowledge that a very small number of US Marines and special forces have been training Taiwanese forces for more than a year – a six-nation joint naval exercise in the Philippine Sea was intended to signal growing allied resolve. Journalist Peter Hartcher wrote in the *Sydney Morning Herald*:

Seventeen naval vessels from six nations ...
conducted joint naval manoeuvres in the Pacific ...
They represented Australia, Canada, Japan, New
Zealand and included US and UK aircraft carrier
strike groups ...

    The senior British officer, Commodore Steve
Moorhouse, said the joint exercise was 'an important
message for those here that nations like ourselves
really do believe in the freedom of navigation, in
the freedom of trade and really are alarmed at the
militarisation of the area. Chinese intelligence-
gathering vessels were in the region, so I have
absolutely no doubt the message would have been
relayed back to China quite quickly.'[3]

In peacetime it is fairly easy for allies, especially from Europe, to agree to conduct these kinds of joint deployments. This jolly attitude to allied solidarity and resolve might not be so obvious if the US's allies were being faced with DF-21D carrier-killer missiles emerging from space at many times the speed of sound, with accuracies of 20 metres, or massive anti-ship cruise missiles fired from H-6 bombers. Or if the Suez and Panama canals had been mined and their infrastructure entirely destroyed.

* * *

Without downplaying the significance of all that is contained in the AUKUS announcements, I do think much more seemed to be publicly ascribed to them than they actually contained. Wishful thinking plus media sensationalism clouds the evidence that a huge amount still needs to be done. The AUKUS agreement is indeed a momentous event for Australia, but despite the popular and media reaction to it, Chinese aggression cannot be considered solved by this announcement alone.

What *is* exciting with regard to AUKUS is that we saw decisive national leadership on defence. The submarines, which may not be in the water for 20 years, are more symbolic of a significant change of attitude than they are an answer to the China problem: a view also put up by many US commentators and serving US naval officers.

But the significance of AUKUS is even wider. It represents a refreshing of the 1951 ANZUS Treaty in that it reminded our major ally, the US, that we are a serious player in Pacific national security, and so refocused the US administration on Australia. It gave us access to US technology, the potential for local missile production, and the possibility of stationing US troops, aircraft, ships and submarines on Australian soil. Overall, it is a mighty signal to China that Australia and its allies are not going to be pushed around.

But there could be a big cost for Australians. As a result of these decisions, which reinforced the togetherness of the three countries involved in AUKUS, it could be considered that Australia is now even more locked into our relationship with the US than we were under ANZUS, which required us to consult in the case of a threat or an attack. AUKUS does not work the same way but it does remind everyone in the world how close we are to the US. This is not something I am uncomfortable with, as long as we realise the limitations of US power and accept our responsibility over the medium to long term to make ourselves self-reliant within that relationship, and do not use the relationship as an excuse not to be self-reliant.

Even after the AUKUS announcements, I stand by my long-held assessment that Australia as a nation remains dangerously vulnerable, and I took Prime Minister Morrison's statement that there were still more things to do as acknowledgement of that situation.

Australia, as a key ally of the US in the region, wields significant diplomatic and political power, and we have seen that in action throughout 2021. Respect for Australia was apparent when Japan asked Australia to lead in the region, and it was Prime Minister Morrison's advocacy that prompted the Quad and AUKUS agreements and meetings.

But in the end only real power matters, which must be the most important lesson from the Ukraine War. Australia's defence potential is significant. We inhabit a single island continent and have no threatening close neighbours. We have a large population that is healthy, well educated and technically oriented. We have natural resources that could make us self-reliant if we chose to be. We are rich and our population is generally well motivated. And we are well governed in comparison with the rest of the world.

Yet our defence potential is far from being realised. Unless Australia adopts emergency measures, such as declaring a defence emergency and then using the powers given to the Commonwealth under the constitution to override, for example, the states' refusal to exploit oil resources under the ground or to ensure the continuation of other energy for industry, we will need years to develop enough military and national power to become self-reliant within these alliances. This is despite the significant steps that the Coalition government took after it came to power in 2013. Every indication is that we may not have years. If this is the case, as I believe it to be and, as we have an obligation to assume it to be, then we should recognise that we are in the early or mid-stages of an emergency situation, and it is legitimate for the Commonwealth to approach the states to cooperate in security aspects and, if they refuse, to claim federal emergency powers. The likelihood that we do not have time to become self-reliant before China challenges the Western Pacific is why I support an even stronger alliance with the US as our only option, particularly in the short to medium term.

As James Curran in *Defense One* argues, 'AUKUS represents the death knell for strategic ambiguity in Australian foreign policy', and that may be a good thing:

> *Although Canberra does have a record of shrewd alliance management in the past – of roaring loud in allied solidarity but committing the minimum muscle up front, as in the case of Iraq 2003 when Australian special forces were pulled back after the initial assault on Baghdad – it is fanciful to suggest that in any future military conflict with China, especially over Taiwan, the United States will not expect Australia to play a role in the battle.*
>
> *Will a future Australian government of either political persuasion be able to resist US pressure to be part of any such conflict? History suggests not. Australia, as we are constantly reminded in the speeches, has been by the US's side at every major conflict since the First World War.*[4]

According to the *South China Morning Post*, a new report released by the Sydney-based United States Studies Centre argues that 'Australian and US military forces should integrate further under a "collective deterrence strategy" aimed at China's rise, giving Canberra access to American operations in the Philippines, Singapore and Guam … The allies should look at new "combined access arrangements" among a number of ways to strengthen "integrated deterrence" against Beijing's growing assertiveness in the region, according to the report.[5] So, an Australian government may at some stage be asked to contribute to a force in the Western Pacific, which may initially be intended to deter China from acting militarily.

In probably the clearest statement on this subject by a senior member of the previous Coalition government, the then Minister for Defence Peter Dutton said that his overriding strategic vision was to make provisions for 'the threat of conflict' in the region and deal with an assertive China by addressing our 'lack of preparedness ... [China's] been very clear about their intent to go into Taiwan and we need to make sure that there is a high level of preparedness, a greater sense of deterrence by our capability, and that is how I think we put our country in a position of strength'.[6]

Mr Dutton noted that China is an economic and military superpower that admits to spending 10 times more a year than Australia on defence, and to producing more military assets by tonnage every 18 months than the Royal Navy has in its current fleet. So the thought that Australia could compete with China 'is of course a nonsense,' he said. 'That's not the question before us; the question is: would we join with the US?'

Mr Dutton added: 'It would be inconceivable that we wouldn't support the US in an action if the US chose to take that action. And, again, I think we should be very frank and honest about that, look at all of the facts and circumstances without pre-committing, and maybe there are circumstances where we wouldn't take up that option, [but] I can't conceive of those circumstances.'[7]

Mr Dutton's comments came after former Labor prime minister Paul Keating told the National Press Club that Taiwan was 'not a vital Australian interest' and not recognised as 'a sovereign state', and that Australia should not be drawn into a conflict over the island.[8] Mr Dutton described Mr Keating as a 'grand appeaser'.[9]

Mr Dutton is right when he speaks of our 'lack of preparedness'. What he means by 'preparedness' is complex. A military can possess certain items of equipment (ships, planes, tanks) which, when they are combined with personnel, training and leadership, produce what is called 'capability'. Capability refers to the ability to actually do something and for a military, that is to fight. For example, a country may have a certain number of warships but, in order to save money in peacetime, the warships may not have their full complement of crew to operate 24 hours a day in a battle situation. The ship may not have the full number of protective weapons to stop missiles because those weapons are expensive; instead of having five missile defence weapons per ship, the ship may only have one which the crew can train on, with the intention of fitting the other four as war approaches. There may also not be enough money in the defence budget to fully train all the crew and to maintain that level of training. So the ship lacks preparedness, as the former minister says.

And that applies across the entire Australian military for every type of equipment and the personnel in every unit. To save money, only some elements of the ADF are kept at full war or operational readiness. This is a legitimate policy whereby the money saved can be spent on buying more equipment with the intention of increasing the readiness of the force as war approaches. The key to this policy is the ability to assess the risk of war early enough to raise the preparedness of all elements of the force. In times of wars of choice, Australia could maintain almost all its force on lower preparedness levels because we knew we could determine when we went to war. In these days, with the possibility of wars of commitment that we must win, where an enemy determines when the war occurs, it is much more difficult to assess risk, and much more important to get preparedness right.

As I have maintained, a war with China is likely to occur any time from now out to three to five years in the future. This is the time Australia and our allies have to develop the capability to counter China, to build more military capability and to raise the level of preparedness of the capability we already have. Three to five years may not be enough. China can be deterred, but that will take real military strength by the US and its allies in the immediate future.

The question that government and military planners must ask is what needs to be done in Australia in the short to medium term – that is, the next five years, the outer limit of my estimated timeframe. Having long-term objectives is commendable, but unlikely to produce results for the next war. Australian national security will be best served if the government takes the right war as the standard it must meet, examines what it needs to do to prepare for that war, and only then decides what risks it can afford to take by *not* preparing.

As I have repeatedly stressed, if there were an understanding of the likely nature of such a war, and a risk analysis were conducted and preparations commenced, Australia should be able to handle anything that the real world throws at us, short of a nuclear war. Sadly, it does not work the other way if Australia prepares only for lesser contingencies like the kind of wars we have been fighting for the last 75 years. In modern war, where decisions are likely to be reached quickly, if we prepare for a lesser contingency we may never get the chance to adjust upwards.

Compared with the likely timeframe for war in our region, Australia's ability to increase our military strength is severely limited. The previous Coalition government claimed that the first of the eight planned nuclear submarines would be 'in the water' by 2039. The US Chief of Naval Operations agreed that the process will take perhaps decades. What has been definitely decided is that there will be an 18-month study, possibly later reduced to 12 months, to identify the details, and that is in train now. The key to making the submarine agreement relevant any time in the next 20 or so years is to identify the proper procurement strategy, and that is what the study will do.

Many, including former prime minister Tony Abbott, are clamouring for nuclear submarines from either the US or the UK to be delivered much earlier than 2039. While the American *Virginia* class submarines are excellent, the US is in no position to shift production efforts and help Australia get started any time soon. Among the biggest challenges is that the US Navy is critically short of submarines itself. It was assumed that certain parts of the *Virginia* attack submarines would last the life of the vessel, but as in-service *Virginia* submarines arrived for maintenance, the navy found it had to replace parts that weren't supposed to need replacing. Since there weren't spares available for these unexpected replacements, maintainers began taking the parts off the production line, thus slowing down production at the only two shipyards building these submarines, General Dynamics Electric Boat and Newport News Shipbuilding. Even if the US could increase nuclear attack submarine production at these shipyards, Washington would likely serve America's needs before Australia's.[10]

The UK, on the other hand, has almost completed its equally excellent *Astute*-class attack submarines. That might leave UK shipyards free to start building *Astute* subs for Australia. The specifics of the nuclear reactor and the front of the submarine where the weapons systems and sensors are – where we may prefer US technology to ease the transition for Australian submariners who primarily operate US systems on the current submarines – could be worked out over the next year.

There is no reason why the Australian government should not try to speed up delivery. Nuclear submarines in two decades' time will be of no value to anyone if war occurs within the next five years. The question is: is it possible to speed up delivery? The answer looks like being no!

As a result, we are likely to fight the China war not with nuclear submarines but with our six diesel–electric, Australian-made *Collins*-class submarines. Given their age and plans for a mid-life update or two, we will probably have only two initially available in the short term, and three or four in an emergency over time.

The decision following the AUKUS announcements to extend the life of the *Collins* class by a decade, from 2030 to 2040 (when the nuclear subs will be in service), revealed in a statement in Senate Estimates by the Australian Chief

Given the long lead time for the delivery of Australia's new nuclear submarines, we are more likely to fight a war with China using our existing *Collins*-class submarines. *(Getty)*

of Navy, seems to have confused commentators and the submarine lobby alike.[11] Certainly, any government needs to explain why it was decided or agreed to in a 2009 defence white paper that we needed 12 submarines then but now we can make do with only six submarines, in a worsening strategic environment, until 2040, at which point we can get away with eight nuclear ones.[12]

Clearly Australia must cover the gap between now and when the nuclear submarines are ready in one or two decades, in part with the *Collins*, but there are other options. It must be remembered that our aim should not just be to *have* submarines. Our aim should be to have the capacity to sink enemy ships and submarines, to lay sea mines, to insert and deploy special forces and to conduct surveillance. All of these tasks can be carried out by aircraft, shore-based missiles or air-dropped sea mines. The only job submarines can do that other forces cannot is a very important one: lurking in an area to establish a persistent presence and make an enemy think that a submarine could be anywhere. A logical plan, derived from an overall defence strategy prepared as a subordinate strategy to a national security strategy, would show the need for more forces to supplement the *Collins* submarines, probably aircraft initially, because they can do most things that a submarine can do, and can be procured much faster than anything else.

This raises the question of what military forces we do have and how effective they are. We have a highly competent and modern military force in Australia which has a good international reputation based on our fighting performance over our history as a nation and, in particular, on our more recent experience in Vietnam, Somalia, Cambodia, East Timor, Iraq and Afghanistan.

It is only possible to judge a defence force against the kind of threats it may have to face, and the Australian military has performed well in all of our wars of choice since the end of World War II because we are good soldiers, sailors and airmen and women, and we have always fought beside our great and powerful ally. I often observe that the ADF has never been better than it is at the moment, particularly with the support and funding it received from the Coalition government from 2013, but that is judging it against the wars of the last 75 years and not against what the ADF may have to do in the future. I stand by the case I made earlier in this book that, despite the advanced nature of our equipment and our moves into cyber and space warfare, the ADF is a one-shot defence force because it lacks lethality (it cannot fight hard enough), sustainability (it cannot fight for long enough) and mass (it is not big enough).

Overall, our navy is very small but attracts a disproportionate amount of examination because of the issue of Australian-built submarines and ships. The previous Coalition government supported the upgrade of navy surface ships and the procurement of destroyers, amphibious ships and logistic support ships, as well as offshore patrol vessels. But the size of the navy needs to be examined, not according to what we think we can afford, but what we need. Regardless, it is very difficult to increase the size of a navy with complex modern ships quickly, as the US is finding out as it tries to grow its navy to match China's navy.

Following their recent upgrades, the Australian navy's eight *Anzac*-class frigates are very capable ships, especially as regards their sensors, especially their radars, but some believe that they need many more missiles on board, in the form of a second eight-cell vertical missile-launching system on each ship. This system, known as the Mark 41 Vertical

Launching System, has missiles preloaded into 'canisters', which are then loaded into the individual 'cells' of the launcher, four to each cell, giving it a total of 32 missiles. These missiles (known as Evolved Sea Sparrow Missiles) protect ships against attacking aircraft or missiles, even supersonic missiles that can manoeuvre to protect themselves as they attack.

The role of these ships is to escort larger vessels in a fleet, convoy or battle group and defend them against short- to medium-range attacks. In the event of hostilities in the Western Pacific, where they are likely to face many Chinese subsonic, supersonic and hypersonic cruise missiles as well as rockets, this small missile-launching capacity is risky to say the least, particularly as the ships have to return to a harbour to reload missiles. Australia's three Air Warfare Destroyers (known as *Hobart* class after the name of the first ship) have 48 vertical launch cells each, but modern US and Chinese ships have twice that number.

In a very good move, the Coalition government planned to acquire the longer-range (some versions exceeding 1000 kilometres) Tomahawk missiles for use on the six *Collins*-class submarines, the three Air Warfare Destroyers and the eight future *Hunter*-class frigates, which will come into service early in the next decade to replace the *Anzac*-class ships. These missiles will all come into service sometime in the future, but unless the new Minister for Defence can work miracles, Australia will not be self-reliant in missile production for the next war.

Our army, like our navy, remains very small. The Coalition government decided to strengthen the army with very capable armoured vehicles, missiles, drones, helicopters and command-and-control IT. But, again, the size of the army is a result of the needs of previous wars and is not related to the wars we may have to fight in the future. In particular, Australia does not have a reserve force, as many other countries have, which, while not as well equipped or as well trained as a full-time army, could be prepared for mobilisation in times of tension.

The air force, meanwhile, is in the process of finishing its purchase of the advanced F-35 fighter aircraft (an aircraft I shall discuss in the next chapter), but of course what our F-35s, our FA-18F Super Hornet fighter–attack aircraft and our Growler EA-18G electronic-warfare aircraft can do is severely limited by the lack of sufficient numbers of refuelling, command-and-control and other specialist supporting aircraft. If we were preparing for the right war, the balance between supporting aircraft and attack aircraft would have been addressed. This imbalance is not a problem for an air force going to a war of choice, but it is a problem for an air force that has to deploy all its assets in an all-out attempt to defend a nation.

Given the size and capability of our military, the question Australian military planners must address in the event of war with China in the Western Pacific is: if Australian ships and planes are sent to a serious fight in the Western Pacific alongside the US, can we afford to lose those ships and planes that are so critical to the defence of our continent, especially if the US is forced out of the Western Pacific for some period? A historical analogy is that in 1940 Australia sent our army to North Africa, our navy to the Mediterranean and our air force to Canada to be trained and then to Europe to fight, when the likelihood of a Japanese attack in our region was well known and subsequently occurred.

So, Australia has enormous defence potential, but fully realising that potential will take time and a total change in national attitude, if we decide to do so, or if we *have* to do so.

* * *

Going to war is a monumental decision and, as such, should not be rushed. The merits of a military contribution by Australia should be very seriously examined as tension builds in the region. In fact, they should be examined by Australia in the greatest detail long before tension occurs. They should be examined now, side by side with the US and other likely allies – Japan and South Korea to begin with – with all options and expectations of our allies on the table.

Our involvement in such a war in China's backyard along with the US should only be agreed upon by Australian authorities if there is more than a fair chance of success against China, and at present the US may not inspire confidence in its allies that there is such a fair chance. The most basic lesson we can learn from our recent involvement in a range of wars is that we, even as a minor ally, need to influence US warfighting strategy, and that needs to occur now, before the build-up to a war begins. Australia must demand a seat at the strategic warfighting table. After all, this is the way NATO works.

Australia also needs to be very clear about *why* we would go to war over Taiwan. The final decision will be taken by the government of the day, but it will not be able to take that decision responsibly at the time unless there has been significant preparation, essentially for years, beforehand. If, of course, we have years.

That preparation would mainly be to create, in the first instance, the physical capability to go to war, that is, weapons and trained personnel backed up by resilience and resolve in the nation. But it would also be necessary to develop a strong mental capacity to go to war, that is, effective and ethical decision-making at government level, supported in execution by resolve among the population.

If we do not have the military capability to go to war effectively, yet do so, that would be truly immoral. Effectiveness in defence in this kind of war is about both protecting our homeland and deploying forces in the Western Pacific along with our allies in order to deter China from attack, or in order to fight if deterrence fails. If Australia were so vulnerable that sending our forces away to war risked bringing down the wrath of a superior enemy on an unprepared nation, that would be very hard to justify. As noted, what Australians generally consider at the moment to be a war in the region of Taiwan might just be the opening battle of a much wider regional war. Later aggression might even be aimed directly at the Australian continent. Because the ADF is essentially a one-shot force, Australia should be very careful about where it deploys that one shot.

Moreover, we only have an obligation to become involved in war only if the war itself is just, and only if we commit to prosecuting such a war in a moral and ethical way. This means we need to make assumptions about the nature of this war and determine whether our involvement would be right. Having run a war in Iraq on that basis, I can only say that the ability to win need not be hampered by prosecuting the war in an ethical way. In fact, to run a war unethically risks losing both the physical and the moral high ground. You *can* win ethically.

To defend Taiwan after China launches a war of aggression is a relatively straightforward moral issue. Opposing aggression is acceptable. To defend Australia if this continent were attacked as part of or after a Taiwan war, which is a distinct possibility, is likewise morally straightforward. Australia is permitted to act in self-defence, even if that self-defence is manifested in offensive ways, such as joining our allies to fight China in the Western Pacific.

But what if the Taiwan war were instigated by an irresponsible attempt by elements in Taiwan to declare independence? Here the issues start to become complex, which is why it is so important to have discussed all aspects of the war far in advance of a time of rising tension, when national leaders may be under extreme pressure.

A response to a war of aggression, past a certain immediate point of self-defence, must be approved by the UN. But what if the aggressor, in this case China, so dominated the UN Security Council that approval by the UN became impossible? Once again, this dilemma should be considered far in advance of the start of any war.

If a nation has decided that it has the capacity to deploy forces to a war while at the same time protecting the homeland because it has created those forces over time, and it has satisfied itself that it is morally justifiable to become involved, a rational nation then needs to ask: is the war winnable? This is particularly important if the war being considered is one involving an existential threat to that country. Again, if there is a lack of confidence that the battles are winnable, much less the war, and that even a stalemate would be too risky for a small nation like Australia, our participation might be morally questionable.

Because of this, the next issue that a responsible government should address is whether to send a token force to such a war to fight beside our allies or send a serious combat force that is committed to winning and is prepared to fight and even to die? Does Australia envisage doing roughly what we have done with our US allies for years – sending a minimal force surrounded by directives and rules of engagement that prevent it from doing any serious fighting, so that the local US commander sees that force as a burden rather than a benefit? Or, alternatively, does Australia send a maximum force to join our allies, one that can fight to win and is prepared to take casualties, unlike every commitment by Australia post-Vietnam?

Given our general relationship with the US, and the new AUKUS alliance in particular, there will be great pressure on Australia to stand beside our ally to the maximum extent, even with the limited military resources we have. We will probably be asked to contribute at least the largest possible air and naval units to a coming war. This pressure will be hard to resist.

If a regional war comes to pass, Australia cannot get away with what we have got away with for decades: sending a minimal force and our national flag, but not sending hard, strong warfighting forces. To deter China – if there is a chance to deploy forces before China attacks, which may not be the case – sending only one token frigate and a few token non-combat aircraft, as we usually do, would make this country a laughing stock in the eyes of our allies. In the next regional war, if there is time, Australia will find that it must commit forces with a view to winning, not just participating as has been our practice for far too long. An existential threat from China requires a committed response by Australia. If Australia does send a substantial force that is prepared to fight and not just show the flag, it is likely that there will be severe casualties. And if the scenario that I predict in this book comes to pass, then many ships and planes will be lost.

It is unlikely that any action Australia might take will ever deter a war between China and the US – we are simply not a big enough player. But if we are to be involved to the extent that we suffer even just collateral damage, we must prepare carefully for two possible outcomes.

The first is the likelihood of an attack on Australia as a US ally – be it by rockets, missiles, sea mines, cyber technology, biological warfare or a trade embargo. Our aim should be to at least reduce our vulnerability to these types of attacks. If we carried out a full strategic assessment, we might discover a large number of deficiencies in this regard. Consequently, we might decide to invest in an ability to defend either the whole nation or the most important parts of the nation against attack by, say, ballistic missiles – we have some relatively important targets on our shores, although missile defence is a very difficult thing to do in a country as big as Australia and might be disproportionately expensive for the return in terms of security.

Alternatively, or in addition, we might increase our capacity to manage a sea-mine attack on our ports, particularly because it might be important for China to limit the ability of Australia to be used as a base for US forces, or it might be of value to China to stop the Australian navy from deploying from its harbours. A consequence of such a sea-mine attack would be that no commercial shipping would be willing to use our harbours because of the danger of losing a ship to a mine or the inability to obtain insurance for a voyage to Australia. Australia is extraordinarily dependent on sea trade even for basic commodities such as liquid fuels, pharmaceuticals, fertilisers and IT, yet it currently has limited ability to clear its ports of modern sea mines. It's said, anecdotally, that only one or two of the seventeen nationally significant ports could be kept open by the Royal Australian Navy.

We could of course improve our resistance to economic attack by producing what we need domestically, such as liquid fuels, by building up a sizeable reserve of fuel or other critical items within the country, and by expanding domestic production of those items in a realistic period of time. That would not mean withdrawing from the global marketplace, but it would mean producing domestically everything we need and not necessarily everything we want. This would require the government to identify critical items and manage the market with controls and subsidies.

Rather than assume that our military forces, mainly navy and air force, would deploy to the vicinity of the first and second island chain to join with a US fleet because that is how we have thought of a Taiwan war for generations, we might decide on a different contribution to a coalition operational plan. We might suggest to the US that Australian forces, along with regional allies such as Indonesia, could control sea and air access through the straits in the Indonesian Archipelago and the South Pacific while at the same time protecting the Australian mainland. This would be achievable, is within the bounds of feasible planning and would be a sensible use of scarce Australian resources. And if the allied war effort were well coordinated, such an Australian operational concept would contribute significantly to the overall war aims.

The second contingency that Australia should prepare for is that the US is forced out of the region by the kind of massive and coordinated surprise attack that I outlined at the start of this book, and Australia then stands alone as an ally of the US in the face of a dominant China, but without US support. To face such a contingency, we would need to be self-reliant, and capable of withstanding China's direct intimidation – even threats of military occupation – or risk becoming a tributary state of China, one that loses its sovereignty because it is required to obey all of China's directions.

* * *

Given the destructive power of modern weaponry, the aim of every person on Earth must surely be to deter war wherever possible. This is why the moral aspect of war is critical. To be able to wage war that involves extreme violence, yet not lose the moral high ground as an individual or as a nation, is an essential way of surviving the most awful of human experiences.

Sadly, over the full expanse of history, war has been one of the most common of human experiences. In the last century, it is estimated that 17 million people died in World War I and then another 60 to 80 million in World War II, and that is not counting the myriad of other wars in places like Korea and Vietnam and Iraq.

War is so appalling that all Australian governments have a solemn responsibility to prepare for it in order to deter it or to minimise its impact should it occur. And the people of Australia should be vitally interested in what their government is doing.

Our world is a tough world, but there are still things in it that are worth making great sacrifices for.

CHAPTER 10

THE RIGHT WAR

What is the right regional war to prepare for, and how should Australia prepare for it? I fail to see how any assessment of Australian defence policies can proceed without a focus on answering these two questions. Preparing for the right war is critically important, because until we understand what a regional war might entail, we have no way of determining whether Australia is effectively defending its sovereignty, the ultimate aim of national security.

As I have been arguing, China has the capability to go to war to achieve its aim of dominance, first in the region and then perhaps across the world, and may do so, and Australia must prepare. The war will be initiated by China at a time of China's choosing. It will be as widespread and as violent as China chooses it to be. China has been preparing for this war for decades and it intends to win.

If a major power like China gets to choose when to initiate hostilities because its major objective is to be the dominant power in the region, it has an enormous, even overwhelming, advantage simply because it has the initiative. China can exercise the advantage that this initiative gives it in one of three main ways:

1. **The incremental model.** This model involves using a wide variety of techniques to pick an issue to advance China's influence and interests – whether it be the building of islands in the South China Sea and the militarisation of those islands; the incorporation of other, mainly developing, countries into China's infrastructure building plans across the world, known as the Belt and Road Initiative, and the use of that influence for military purposes, as in the South Pacific; the suppression of dissent in Hong Kong; skirmishes on the Sino-Indian border in the Ladakh; cyber activity and the theft of intellectual property from foreign companies and universities; the use of social media to create distrust of institutions in other countries; the weaponisation of trade; and attempts to extend influence by bribing decision-makers in foreign countries. The essence of the incremental model is that no one activity

is enough to cause a significant reaction from
the target countries, but put together they have
a real benefit for China. Should any of the target
countries react to any of the increments, then
China denies involvement, lies about the issue and/
or rapidly backs off. In many of these spheres,
China achieves its objectives without causing a
dramatic reaction from any of the target countries
and, when there is a reaction, it is usually mainly
rhetorical. Behind the incremental moves there
is always the implied threat of direct military
action by China, which is one reason why target
countries are cowed.

2. **The sudden-attack model.** This model involves
the sudden and violent use of military might,
with the intention of achieving a decisive result,
at least in the short to medium term. This model
only became viable for China in the past decade
or so because for many decades prior to the
early twenty-first century, the power of the US
effectively deterred such a move. China's advances
in space technology, cyber warfare, nuclear
weaponry, rocketry, missiles and conventional
military forces (ships, planes and tanks) mean
that this option can now be considered. What has
also made this model viable is the reduction in US

military power since the end of the Cold War in 1991 (discussed previously), and a perception that the West is in decline and US leadership is weak. This model depends very heavily on surprise and every effort would be made to not signal that a sudden attack was imminent.

3. **The combination model.** As the name suggests, this is a combination of the incremental and the sudden-attack models. China would continue to use the incremental approach, taking smaller, apparently unconnected steps to either achieve its objectives without the costs of a major war, if that were possible, or, over a longer period, it might act incrementally to create the conditions for a sudden attack if the incremental approach was not bringing about regional dominance. When China was ready or when there was an opportunity, then it would suddenly attack. The incremental model was used by Germany prior to World War II, when it employed both diplomacy and coercion throughout the 1930s to take advantage of European naïveté and post–World War I war weariness. Violent armed force was not employed by Germany until it had built up its military to a necessary strength, and when the likelihood of achieving its objectives by incremental methods

had diminished. This resulted in an incremental
gaining of Germany's strategic objectives, always
with the option of backing off if it overreached
and met with more opposition than expected.

A comparison of China with Nazi Germany serves to illuminate this argument. China has already embarked on a version of the incremental model, building over time on its grey-zone activities as a means of weakening and intimidating the US and its regional allies, while making real territorial gains, just as Germany did. All of the grey-zone methods China has utilised are incremental techniques based on bullying and coercion, backed up by the threat of China's massive armed forces.

China has positioned itself well through these grey-zone operations and thinks that the US and its allies – which as I have said it believes are weak and in decline – have been successfully cowed. (This is why the AUKUS agreement is so important: to demonstrate to China that there is resolve in the region.)

In the vicinity of Taiwan, China has recently been carrying out various intimidatory activities as part of its grey-zone strategy, such as regularly flying large numbers of attack aircraft across the centre line of the Air Defence Identification Zone (ADIZ) between Taiwan and China. Chinese air force flights towards or past Taiwan increased through 2021 and 2022, with periods of near-daily flights, usually involving a small number of planes, though in mid-2022 even attack helicopters were used. In addition to air incursions against Taiwan, China has been conducting amphibious exercises in the area as well naval live-firing exercises. It has also conducted almost daily transgressions of Japan's airspace, requiring the dispatch of Japanese fighter aircraft to intercept the Chinese aircraft and escort them out of the area. While these activities have been increasing generally, large incursions usually appear to be in response to particular events, for instance US arms sales to Taiwan, or military activity by Taiwan in or near the Taiwan Strait.

Perhaps the upper limit of the incremental option for China, just short of the use of armed force, would be to declare a no-fly, no-sail exclusion zone around Taiwan based on some pretext, to be subsequently enforced by Chinese air and sea forces. Such an exclusion zone would prevent all aircraft and ships, military and civilian, from entering or leaving. China would have to deploy a credible military presence prepared to use force, including the sinking of ships and the shooting down of aircraft, to maintain the zone. Academic Peter Layton writes:

The final trend is that having undertaken apparently successful grey-zone activities, China may use the

technique elsewhere including against Taiwan ...
President Xi Jinping will not leave the unification
of the mainland and Taiwan to future generations.
While large-scale military conflict is improbable ...
a more likely scenario is a protracted and intensive
campaign by Beijing, using 'all means short of war'.
A grey-zone operation could be commenced that
aims to destabilize Taiwanese society and force its
government to enter into unification talks.[1]

A no-fly, no-sail exclusion zone around Taiwan would technically constitute an act of war and would permit the US and its allies to use force to counter it if they thought themselves strong enough. Given this, China could wait to see how Taiwan and the world reacted while slowly bankrupting Taiwan. If China encountered more resolve in its opponents than expected – which at the moment does not look likely – it could either back off or, if it were sufficiently prepared and wished to do so, rapidly move to the full use of armed force.

If the US decided to do nothing except protest, boycott, sanction and attempt resolution through the UN, China would use its influence at the UN, where it controls many of the international bodies, to delay any counter-action. US credibility would be increasingly diminished the longer it failed to act, while Taiwan would come slowly under China's control. And if Australia did not insist on being part of the US decision-making process in the leadup to such events, we would deserve the insecurity we would then face.

The sudden-attack model was used by the Japanese when they attacked Pearl Harbor: a surprise assault out of a clear blue sky, delivering a devastating blow, from which it was hoped the US would not be able to recover until imperial Japan had consolidated and fortified its gains as far south as the Dutch East Indies. If China decides to take sudden, direct and, it would hope, decisive military action in the immediate future rather than rely on incremental grey-zone action over time, it is likely to do so only in its own backyard, where its military strength is most pronounced and where the US is weakest. China would want to have all the advantages, especially short lines of supply and the ability to quickly magnify its military strength.[2]

Based on its assessment of its opponents, China could act with little or no warning, as Japan did in 1941, or it could manufacture a reason to act. For example, it could take advantage of arrangements such as the 20-year-old Sino–Russian Treaty of Friendship, addressing 'defence of national unity and territorial integrity', which was extended for a further five years in mid-2021. Meeting just prior to the February 2022 Winter Olympics, President Putin and President Xi reaffirmed their relationship, declared their opposition to any expansion of NATO, and affirmed that the island of Taiwan is part of China. Their 5000-word joint statement also highlighted what they called 'interference in the internal affairs' of other states. Ironically, this declaration was made as Russia assembled its military forces around the border of Ukraine, and just before the invasion of that country by Putin's forces. Reports claimed that Xi asked Putin to delay military action against Ukraine until the Beijing Winter Olympics had concluded. The Winter Olympics finished on 20 February. On 21 February Putin sent his troops into the two disputed provinces in the Donbas, and on 24 February the Russian invasion began in earnest. The message to the world, especially to the US, was clear: don't interfere in Ukraine or, by implication, in Taiwan if something should happen, and be aware that China and Russia stand shoulder to shoulder.

A sudden Chinese attack in the Indo-Pacific region could feasibly be coordinated with Russia and/or other allies such as Iran, North Korea and Venezuela; however, there is no indication of that being likely at the moment but it must be planned for.

Any reduction of the US presence in the Western Pacific might also encourage China to launch a sudden attack. Such a reduction could stem from events almost anywhere in the world – for example, if the US redeployed Pacific forces to support Ukraine in its ongoing war with Russia, or if, say, Iran closed the Persian Gulf, thereby suspending all oil shipments to US allies such as Australia. The US and its allies might then send military forces to open that seaway.

The sudden-attack option could gradually come to be seen as a preferable alternative to the incremental model if China observes continued weak US and allied responses to its grey-zone activities, or if it becomes aware that it cannot achieve its objectives by incremental methods. Such a course of action would be very high risk, but it could potentially bring very high rewards for China, so it will always be enticing – just as the Japanese considered the planned attack on Pearl Harbor very high risk, but still went ahead with it. Given the potential for a sudden attack, Australian planners must focus on this worst-case but logical scenario, regardless of how much more comforting it might be to dwell on less-demanding scenarios.

* * *

In the vast Indo-Pacific region, the US military depends on a complex of air and naval bases, a wide range of support aircraft and ships, intelligence gained from satellites, and a communications network capable of receiving and distributing large quantities of data to and from headquarters and allies. Combined with the warships and combat aircraft that carry the attack to an enemy, or defend US and allied interests in the Pacific and the Indian oceans, this results in an enormous US military force of 375,000 personnel, known as the Indo-Pacific Command, or USINDOPACOM. It is this force that makes the US the dominant regional power.

To defeat this kind of military capability even just in the Western Pacific, an enemy such as China would have to attack the bases, the aircraft and ships, but also critical infrastructure such as fuel and communications to reduce the ability of the US and its allies to reinforce the Western Pacific from the continental US or anywhere else in the world. And China would have to attack in a way that did not cause the US, if it suffered such a defeat, to use its overwhelming number of nuclear weapons as a first (nuclear) strike against China.

Something as complex as this military command inevitably has a number of vulnerable nodes. The Indo-Pacific Command is of course, dependent on the intelligence that it gets from space through a range of satellites and also from space-based communications, through which it receives directions from Washington and disseminates its own orders to subordinate elements across half the world. This is backed up by civilian seabed cables which carry encrypted military data, plus there are backup systems often based on high-frequency radio, to be used if all others fail. Because of the nature of radio waves, these backup systems have very limited bandwidth and so are slow in transmitting data. The internet, which is carried primarily through seabed cables, is very important for the military, but it is not just the cables that are vulnerable, it is the ability of an enemy to get into and distort all parts of the cyber system.

The regional US bases, which are airfields, harbours, armouries (missile storage facilities), fuel storage and other facilities, being geographically fixed and poorly hardened and defended, are particularly vulnerable. Most vulnerable are the ships in harbour and the aircraft on the airfields. It is much easier to destroy these assets when they are in their bases rather than at sea or in the air, if of course you can reach them with something accurate enough and powerful enough. Navy fleets at sea used to be able to hide in the vastness of an ocean and manoeuvre to protect themselves. Nowadays they may have lost some of that protection given the development of long-range missiles whose paths can be continually corrected mid-flight and which, it is maintained, have a degree of accuracy that can hit and kill a US aircraft carrier.

So, in summary, the most vulnerable parts of US military power in the Indo-Pacific are: space-based communications; seabed cables; backup systems; cyber systems; bases; aircraft and ships in or on their bases; and naval fleets at sea. Should China be able to destroy or neutralise US power in the Western Pacific by attacking these vulnerable points, it is fair to say the US would lose its power and influence, and China would become the dominant regional power. If the US wanted to make a fight of it, as it did after Pearl Harbor, then the US would need to re-establish its power somewhere in the region, use that as its base and then fight back, as it did with Australia in World War II.

Because of the critical role that allies of the US play in providing bases for US forces in the Western Pacific, China would need to somehow assure itself that it could convince these allies not to fight on once the US was unable to back them militarily. In my view, Japan and South Korea are far too close to China to fight on by themselves without the US, as well as having other enemies in the region who would like nothing better than to see them both reduced by China. It can therefore be assumed that these countries would at least listen to a Chinese proposition such as 'Let's not fight, let's trade and all of us Asians be prosperous together now that the US is gone.'

Taiwan is even closer to the source of Chinese military power than Japan or South Korea, and without US backing is hardly defendable at all, so any proposition from China would at that stage be attractive to any Taiwanese government. 'Return to the fold,' China might say, 'and look forward to a prosperous future as a prosperous autonomous region within the PRC. If you do not return, we will destroy you and reduce anyone who is left to poverty, and then occupy you.'

Australia is further away from China than the other allies, but its lack of military power in the absence of the US makes it just as vulnerable. If the US decided to fight back against China following the kind of defeat in the Western Pacific I have described, Australia, along with Hawaii and Alaska, would be ideal bases from which to mount a counter-offensive. The critical questions would be how long it would take for the US to build up its strength in the Pacific again and could Australia last as an independent country for that period with China rampant in the region?

So, if China decided to go to war, it would have to do a number of things simultaneously and completely.

- Launch offensive operations in space (possibly assisted by Russia or others) to ensure maximum destruction of US and allied reconnaissance and communications satellites (both military and civilian), either by jamming them or by destroying them by denying entire orbits to US satellites, smashing them to bits or burning their electronic parts with space- and ground-based lasers. These operations would probably have to be repeated as soon as the US and its allies managed to relaunch replacement satellites. At the same time, China would need to protect its own satellites against US and allied attacks.
- Launch massive cyber-attacks on the civil and military networks of the US and key allies around

the world, again assisted by its few allies, closing
down industry, logistics and communications.
The US and its allies would try to recover their
internet systems and networks in the days after
such an attack, new satellites would be launched –
and in fact some are kept standing by for just this
purpose – but they would be few, and Earth-based
systems would be repaired where possible. China
would hope to achieve at least a few days' worth
of massive disruption before the networks could be
even partially re-established.

- Launch maximum missile and rocket attacks
on US air and naval bases in Japan, South
Korea, Guam, possibly Diego Garcia, and even
command-and-control facilities in countries such
as Singapore and Australia. China would hope to
achieve the destruction of all the ships and planes
on those bases and in the harbours and also, by
attacking the key infrastructure described above,
prevent the US using those bases for many weeks
to support replacement aircraft and ships.

- Strike US fleet units at sea in the first and second
island chains with onshore carrier-killer missiles at
longer ranges or with land-based anti-ship missiles
for US vessels closer to shore, as well as missiles
launched from aircraft.

- Activate its own air-defence system on the
  mainland in anticipation of counterattacks on its
  bases by any regional enemy forces that might
  have survived. If China's surprise attack was even
  partially successful, then very few allied attack
  aircraft or tankers would remain. This system
  would include long-range air-to-air missiles
  launched against any surviving US strike or tanker
  aircraft, any navy aircraft that might have been
  launched off aircraft carriers that were able to
  operate and were within range, or against aircraft
  that might have been rapidly brought into the
  region.

- Attack the US nuclear submarines that are
  normally stationed in the vicinity of the Taiwan
  Strait and openly acknowledged by the US because
  the role of these submarines, ironically given our
  scenario, is to deter Chinese action.

- Order its own submarines to conduct cruise-
  missile attacks on key regional targets and sea-
  mine warfare against key shipping lanes and
  regional harbours, including places as distant as
  Australia, to slow down the ability of the US and
  its allies to redeploy forces. China would also
  have the option of blocking transit routes such as
  the Suez Canal using civilian ships, which would

hamper the US's European allies or European-
based US forces from redeploying to the Pacific,
and take weeks to be cleared.

Once the success of China's strikes in space, in cyberspace and on US bases in Japan, South Korea and Guam was confirmed, and US submarine strength in the Taiwan area was eliminated or reduced so that it posed no more than a reasonable risk to Chinese ships, China would probably move small groups of forces by air to the edge of the first island chain and occupy key points with land-based anti-ship and anti-air missiles and early-warning forces, to pre-empt the seizure of similar points by US forces and prevent the ingress of a US fleet to within the first island chain, from where effective air and missile attacks could be mounted. A major advantage of this move for China would be that any ensuing naval battle – if there were one, and it would appear in this scenario to be unlikely – would start several thousand kilometres off China's coast.

As soon as it was relatively safe to do so, China would move its surface fleets from their secure bases on the mainland to within the first island chain, essentially into the East and South China seas. From there, China would use every opportunity to attack any US ships that approached from within the second island chain (of which there should not be many left), using missiles from these ships; shore-based missiles now located on the key points within the first island chain; submarines; long-range aircraft firing cruise missiles; and long-range rockets and missiles launched from the mainland.

With its defensive perimeter consolidated in the first island chain and giving it control of adjacent seas, and the US submarine threat reduced, China would be in a position to begin a full air and sea invasion of Taiwan if it still needed to, and, if it did invade, China would be able to limit the casualties and destruction that might previously have been involved. In its new position of strength, it might then move to offer other countries in the region a prosperous and secure future, protected by China's military and its economic strength – as long as they did not resist.

CHAPTER 11

CAN THE US WIN?

China has spent decades preparing for a war in its backyard, and at present it is likely to win – at least in the short to medium term. This is admitted by the US military and informed commentators, but the logical consequences have not yet entered Australia's consciousness.

Unless we have an understanding of the nature of a likely regional war – that is, timings, speed and activities – how is it possible to prepare? Would Australian warships be able to clear mines from Sydney Harbour before the most critical phase of such a war was over? Would NATO be able to make ready and send forces halfway across the world before everything was over? Would the US be able to send more aircraft or ships from distant bases in Hawaii and Alaska, and would it still have the regional bases to send them to? Realistically, if China succeeded with a surprise attack like the scenario I have outlined in this book, all current operational concepts that exist in the Australian military, and in the minds of our national leadership, would be useless.

The scenario I have put forward will be disputed by those who find it intimidating because of set beliefs, based on ignorance and well-intentioned hope, in the limited nature of a war between the US and China over Taiwan. These people desperately hope that China will act stupidly.

It may be that China would try to incorporate Taiwan by force in a militarily unsound way, by leaving US forces in place in regional countries and on the high seas, but China has put an enormous amount of its national treasure and decades of effort into building a rocket and missile force designed to do exactly what my scenario envisages. Why would they not use it? China could launch its amphibious fleet across the Taiwan Strait into the teeth of missile attacks not just from Taiwanese forces, but also from US submarines, while fending off US air and surface fleet attacks. But where is the logic in that?

China might very well decide to signal its intent to use military force by aggressive rhetoric or by assembling its forces around mainland bases that can be surveilled by satellites, just as the Russian forces were continually surveilled as they assembled around the Ukraine border for weeks before the invasion, thus allowing Ukraine and its supporters to prepare military force and sanctions. If China assembled conventional military invasion forces, air forces and amphibious ships along the mainland coast opposite Taiwan, or as close as it could get to Japan and South Korea, and so allowed the US and its allies to concentrate their forces to counter an attack, or temporarily move their vulnerable forces in vulnerable bases out of harm's way, then China would deserve to suffer the best that the US could throw at it.

Some argue that China might very well decide that it wants to avoid the level of US enmity that would result from an attack on US bases in the region and the casualties that would occur, and instead would be more likely to conduct a conventional sea-borne D-Day-style attack. But how much less would the US hate China for such an attack on Taiwan compared to the scenario I propose in this book? And even if the US's hate for China in response to a sudden attack on US bases and the removal of US power from the Western Pacific was far greater, sadly, the US could still do nothing militarily about it because the US and its allies would no longer have forces intact in the region.

China may act stupidly when it actually does not have to do so, when there is an alternative that delivers it both Taiwan *and* regional dominance. Then again, it may not.

* * *

Should my suggested scenario occur, or something very like it, it is hard to see that the UK at least would not support the US, at least diplomatically. But the question is whether European countries would be prepared to send armed forces halfway around the world to fight against a China empowered by its successful sudden attack, beside a weakened and humiliated America which has lost its bases in the region, some ships, and many of its aircraft, and left regional allies questioning how the war might end.[1]

As I have discussed, why would China give the world time to assemble US, and particularly NATO forces, to confront it? The whole purpose of a surprise attack would be to deny the target of that attack time to prepare. As suggested above, if China acted in a logical manner from a military point of view, it would have consolidated its hold on the first and second island chains long before European ships had passed through the Suez Canal. And why would they leave the Suez Canal open to shipping, knowing how easy it is to close the canal, particularly after seeing how, in March 2021 a container ship accidentally jammed itself across the canal and blocked the main channel of the canal for three months?

The military involvement of European or even regional allies like Australia would require a build-up of tension that prompted the early deployment of allied sea and air fleets from various parts of the world. If China is half smart, which it is, it will avoid putting the world on notice. Even Australia, regardless of our intent, might miss the war, given the current unpreparedness of our military, and the distance from Australia to likely combat zones.

* * *

There are probably good reasons why word has leaked from classified US wargames addressing the Taiwan scenario. The US military wants at least a chance to win, and undoubtedly thinks they are not getting it from Congress.

These wargames are very serious activities, which the Americans run very well. They are not scripted as some training wargames might be in order to achieve certain training aims but are played against a 'live' enemy, called a Red Team, who use innovative but real-world tactics and are unpredictable, just as war is and just as our enemies are likely to be.

Apparently, the way the US has tried to fight these in these wargames has not given commanders any confidence that the US could prevail against China. In crude terms, on each occasion – so the leaks go – the US 'has been handed its arse'. We have not been informed of the detail of these games. We do not know exactly what scenario the wargames were based on. Regardless, the US military does not believe it can win by fighting a war in China's backyard with the forces it currently has.

These wargame losses convinced the Vice Chairman of the US Joint Chiefs of Staff, General John Hyten, in mid-

2021, to abandon the warfighting concepts that had guided US military operations for decades. He reported: 'Without overstating the issue, it failed miserably. An aggressive Red Team that had been studying the United States for the last 20 years just ran rings around us. They knew exactly what we were going to do before we did it.'[2] Among the game's lessons: first, the US doctrine of massing forces is a recipe for 21st-century defeat; second, the information networks that define modern American warfare will disappear almost instantly once combat begins. Massing forces might, in a Taiwan scenario, refer to the concentration and dependence of warfighting forces on and around a few US bases in the region, which if they were destroyed would represent a massive loss for the US. The information networks that Hyten refers to are heavily dependent on space and on cyberspace, which in turn are vulnerable to a sudden Chinese attack. This is the essence of the correct war that we should be preparing for.

In response, since October 2021, the Joint Chiefs of Staff have been shifting the US military to a new concept of warfighting operations they call 'Expanded Maneuver'. Unfortunately the concept has been described using the worst kind of military jargon, making it hard to understand what it consists of. Essentially, it seems to involve four ideas: keeping war fighters supplied with fuel and other items no matter where they are nor how dispersed they might be (referred to as Contested Logistics); being able to bring the fires of widely dispersed units, whether part of the army, navy or the air force, onto a single target (Joint Fires); connecting all devices to find targets (referred to as sensors) through superior communication, to enable better decisions to be made faster (Joint All-Domain Command and Control); and sharing real-time information and data across the entire force, including allies (Information Advantage).

The US wants its military to be ready to fight under the new operating concept by 2030, using many of today's weapons, aircraft and ships, but pulled together in a new way that avoids the pitfalls revealed in the wargames. But can it do it in China's backyard, and does it have until 2030 to fix its problems?

It is only prudent to consider in any planning scenario that China will probably *not* play the game in accordance with our preconceived ideas. It will probably *not* give warning of an attack by raising tensions and so allowing forces to be assembled against it from across the world. It will probably *not* visibly assemble any invasion forces that can be detected by foreign surveillance and provide a reason for us to act against it. Yet, current military thinking, particularly in Australia, assumes that there will be a rise in tension, China's forces will assemble somewhere on the mainland, the defences of Taiwan will be worn down to a certain extent, air-defence zones will be established around Taiwan and around China's mainland bases to protect them from US attacks, the invasion of Taiwan will occur by air and sea, the US will intervene from its bases and from aircraft carriers, and someone will win and someone will lose or there will be a stalemate, and all of this without a nuclear exchange.

This is too convenient and comfortable ever to happen.

Even before the wake-up call of recent defeat in the wargames occurred, and the search for a new US fighting concept was endorsed at the highest US command level, the US had considered a range of tactical concepts that might work to assist in the defence of Taiwan. Some of these have been touched on earlier, but I will revisit them here, so that we can then focus on preparing for the right war.

The US has long considered using so-called tripwire forces located in Taiwan, which would report if an attack were imminent and call in reinforcements. But while several decades ago, the US might have been able to move hundreds of thousands of troops unhindered across the Atlantic to Europe or across the Pacific to Korea, today China's dominant capability in certain classes of rockets and missiles, as well as the reach of its rapidly developing submarine and air forces, makes reinforcing Taiwan in the leadup to a war, or once a war has started, an activity of great risk, and perhaps even impossible.

The deterrent capability of US submarines in the vicinity of the Taiwan Strait used to be considered the classic asymmetric defence. This is because for just one or two boats, a small commitment, each of which can carry up to 50 land or ship attack missiles and can be located somewhere within about 1000 kilometres of the strait, the US could deter a Chinese invasion fleet. But, as I shall discuss in more detail later, the value of these submarines is likely to become limited by China's steadily improving anti-submarine capability.

The US has also considered relying on US or allied land forces stationed permanently on Taiwan, as part of Taiwan's permanent defence structure. But there is no desire now to take over the defence of Taiwan from the Taiwanese, especially after the US experience in Iraq and Afghanistan and with Ukraine fresh in everyone's minds. So other solutions need to be found.

China's anti-access, area-denial strategy (called A2/AD) – its strategy to prevent US forces from penetrating the first island chain – would predominantly use its rocket, missile and submarine forces, stationed in the first island chain, to target the major surface elements of the US fleet: its aircraft and helicopter carriers and its Aegis destroyers.[3] The US understands that if the US fleet in the first and second island chains loses major ships or submarines, and US regional bases are attacked at the same time, the US will have little choice but to leave the Western Pacific and relocate any forces that are left to Hawaii, Alaska or as far south as Australia.

To target so accurately, China would depend on its space-based surveillance satellites and its over-the-horizon radars (more on them later), plus the ability to correct the course of certain missiles during their flight. This applies especially to the DF-21D, the nuclear or conventionally armed missile referred to as the 'carrier killer', which has a range of over 2000 kilometres and an accuracy of 20 metres,[4] and to another longer-range missile, the DF-26, referred to as the 'Guam killer'. Bases closer to China such as those in the Japanese Ryukyu Islands and the Philippines would be particularly exposed.

Given the formidable power of China's rocket and missile force, the US military and Congress are right to be concerned about the vulnerability of their bases in the Western Pacific. But, according to a report on *Defense News*, the US has not yet advanced past rather pathetic 'interim solutions':

The US Army will send to Guam one of the two Iron Dome air-and-missile defense batteries it recently purchased as an interim solution for cruise-missile defense, according to an Oct. 7 statement from the 94th Army Air and Missile Defense Command.

The deployment, dubbed Operation Iron Island, will test the capabilities of the system and further train and refine the deployment capabilities of air defenders, the statement notes. It will also fulfill the requirement in the fiscal 2019 National Defense Authorization Act that an Iron Dome battery be deployed to an operational theater by the end of 2021.[5]

The US is trying to be innovative at the tactical and operational levels, adopting tactics such as loading F-15E fighter jets up with cruise missiles to see if they can be used like bombers. But every single innovation depends on secure regional bases from which such power can be projected. US regional bases are the Achilles heel in a regional war, and Australian forces would be just as vulnerable as those of the US if we elected to station our forces in the same places.

In any coming conflict, air power will be critical, therefore bases will be critical.[6] One thing that the US (and Australia) is very good at is the coordination of large numbers of aircraft of different types, called packages, to strike different targets in a coordinated 'air war'. This is something that the US and its allies have developed over many decades in their Middle East wars, and which Australia has experienced and learned from. The two allies operate common software and communications systems and share common ways of doing things, referred to as doctrine.

If the US were to encounter a situation in which it was appropriate or possible to attack Chinese sea and air bases on the mainland, and US aircraft and bases had not been previously destroyed by a sudden Chinese attack, the US Air Force would need to attack all or most of China's hardened coastal air and naval bases not just once, but perhaps several times. Because the very few regional US air bases that exist are remote compared with the many Chinese coastal air bases, a serious US strike would require a large number of refuelling tanker aircraft waiting several hundred kilometres off the Chinese coast to refuel strike packages as they went in and came out.

As discussed earlier, these 'tanker lines' would be a prime target for China's air-launched long-range missiles. If US launching bases had not yet been attacked, it might be possible for fighter aircraft to get into China's air bases on the first occasion, perhaps using stealth, but they would be unlikely to make it back to their bases if the tanker aircraft were destroyed. It would then be even harder for them to hit Chinese targets a second time.

As well as requiring tanker support within a few hundred kilometres of their operational areas, many US jets in the Pacific need a range of other support aircraft to operate at their maximum effectiveness. They need command-and-control aircraft, electronic warfare and intelligence-gathering aircraft, and heavy-lift aircraft to support the logistic train. Take away the command-and-control and electronic-intelligence aircraft, all of which depend on very sophisticated US bases and large amounts of fuel to travel across the vast Pacific, and things get very difficult. Take away the tanker aircraft to refuel the strike packages and the mission is over. Take away the air bases through Chinese rocket and missile attack and the mission never starts.

The question continually returns to the security of bases. There have been calls for almost a decade for much more money to be spent on hardening US bases to make them less vulnerable. Some work has been done but nothing compared with the efforts China has put in. Its military is based in up to 40 hardened air and naval bases in areas on its coast that have good access to Taiwan, and many of its 3210 aircraft can be hidden and protected in underground tunnels. This disparity is compounded by the warning and strike power of the artificial islands in the South China Sea that China has created illegally.

Particular concern has been publicly expressed about the vulnerability of the giant Andersen Air Force Base on Guam, and the need for the US Congress to fund an air-defence system known as Aegis Ashore, adapted from the Aegis Ballistic Missile Defense System used by the US (and Australian) Navy.[7] Back in 2018, when one particular unclassified study was done, China had hundreds of cruise missiles and 1400 ballistic missiles; now it has at least

2000 ballistic missiles. Most have a range of less than 1000 kilometres, but China also has more intermediate-range missiles (1000 to 3000 kilometres) that can reach Japanese bases with an accuracy of 5 to 10 metres, and a lesser number of long-range missiles. The Chinese are more than capable of causing enough destruction to close US air or naval bases – for example, Kadena on Okinawa, home to 20,000 US personnel – for an indeterminate period.

* * *

In 2018, global thinktank the RAND Corporation assessed that China has the advantage over the US in its ability to penetrate and attack US air bases. In the case of valuable fighter aircraft such as the F-22 and F-35, and their key support aircraft, it is not about technology as much as it is simply about the numbers.

So how *does* US air strength stack up against China's? Accurate numbers of China's aircraft are harder to get hold of than those of US aircraft. In the US F-22 fighter class, China operates about 100 J-20 fighters, with some analysts saying the numbers may be closer to 200. This compares with 125 US F-22 aircraft in fighting squadrons, of which 60% are available at any one time for combat – that is, 75 aircraft.

China also has at least 300 different Soviet 'Flanker'-type aircraft of various vintages and variants, roughly

China has at least 300 different Soviet 'Flanker'-type aircraft of various vintages and variants, roughly equivalent to a US F-15. *(Getty)*

equivalent to a US F-15. The F-15 is an older (first entered service in 1972), rugged, twin-engine, air-superiority fighter with over 100 air victories and no losses which has been developed most successfully as a strike aircraft capable of attacking ground targets. The US operates around 400 of several variants of F-15s, including 165 of the latest Strike Eagle version, the F-15E.

China's J-10 series aircraft is the equivalent of the US F-16 class, which is a multi-role aircraft (meaning it is able to fight other aircraft as well as carry out ground-attack missions), smaller than the F-15, with one engine and relatively short range. About 4600 have been built since 1976 and the plane is in service with 25 countries. The US Air Force operates 1245 F-16s, of which 700 would be immediately available for combat across the world, with 544 in the Air National

Guard and the Reserve, consisting of part time personnel. China intends to build around 1000 J-10 aircraft.

Evidently, China's air force is comparable in numbers of quality fighters in the given tiers explained. With regard to a conflict in the Western Pacific, it would also have the advantage of a concentrated air fleet, whereas US fleets are spread paper-thin across the US and on overseas deployments, and its F-15 and F-16 fleets are mostly around 30 years of age.

The US F-22 fighter aircraft is a key part of the US warfighting equation, as probably the best aircraft of its type in the world. It is a valuable warfighting tool, but it is poorly suited to very long range operations, having been designed to operate from European bases that have far more support assets and not as much need for refuelling tankers. The US Air Force has been starved of funds for F-22 maintenance, upgrades and spare part stocks over the last decade or so, so combat availability is perhaps 60% of the 186 F-22 aircraft in existence. This would not be an issue if fleet numbers were not already so low. The overall number of F-22s is too small to allow for the concentration of force required to deal with the most sophisticated Chinese aircraft. No more F-22s can afford to be lost – much less lost on the ground, on bases that are inadequately hardened.

Of the 186 F-22 jets in existence, only about 125 of them are assigned to combat squadrons, with the rest being set aside for various training and test and evaluation duties. Many of the jets in the latter categories have not been upgraded to the most recent standard. So, there are very few of these top-line aircraft compared to the number of aircraft China operates, their maintenance system is deficient in the region, they are not long-range fighters and need tanker support, and when they are on the ground in undefended bases they are particularly vulnerable. This is not a situation designed to create confidence in warfighting leaders or in allies.

The more modern F-35 fighter aircraft, still being introduced into service, is touted as the most lethal, survivable and connected fighter aircraft in the world. The

The US F-35 fighter is a very impressive aircraft, but it currently lacks the range, performance and stealth capability that would be required for a war in the Western Pacific. *(Getty)*

term 'connected' means the F-35 is connected to other sources of data indicating targets and threats and is thereby part of a much larger system rather than just a single aircraft. It is also a multi-role aircraft, meaning it can fight against other aircraft (in air-to-air combat, as the saying goes), carry out surveillance and attack ground targets. It has extensive stealth characteristics too, allowing it to minimise detection by enemy radar.

Only 720 of these aircraft had been built and brought into full service as of March 2022, with a plan to produce 175 per year. At present, they are spread over 13 countries, not all of whom would join the US in a war against China. The majority are held by the US, with the air force planning to ultimately have 1763 of them, the US Marines 420 and the US Navy 273. This compares to the very large numbers of Chinese aircraft with only one operator – the PLA air force – which operates them from hardened bases backed up by an apparently functioning maintenance system under, one assumes, a single plan as to how they should be used.

The F-35 comes in three variants. The F-35A is a conventional take-off and landing aircraft using long concrete runways. (The Royal Australian Air Force currently has 44 of these aircraft, and aims to have 72 operational by 2023 and ultimately 100 in total.) The F-35B model is a short take-off and vertical landing aircraft suitable for restricted airfields, smaller aircraft carriers and helicopter carriers, and it can also be deployed away from main bases to make it less vulnerable. (It is operated by, among others, the US Marine Corps and the Royal Navy.) The F-35C is designed to operate from larger aircraft carriers, such as the supercarriers operated by the US Navy.

Although a very impressive aircraft, at this stage the F-35 lacks the range, performance and stealth capability to be as effective as may be necessary. Like all such US aircraft designed for the European theatre, it is unsuited to combat involving the vast distances of the Pacific because of its short range, though there is talk of longer-range variants to come. In addition, the fleet availability of the F-35 is below 50%, and at one stage there were no fewer than 21 different configurations, each with substantially unique hardware and software. Throughout the US F-35 fleet, spare parts often have to be manufactured to order, which can take many months. For the kind of combat operation that we may see in the Pacific against China, the problem is compounded by the need for long concrete runways, at least for the F-35A; deploying them out of forward-operating bases, such as highways in remote areas, is extremely difficult.

The Next Generation Air Dominance (NGAD) fighter, which will eventually succeed the F-22, is still in the conceptual stage and too far away to be counted, which is why commentators speak of the 'fighter capability gap' between the US and its likely adversaries, primarily China, in the next decade or so. This is a real gap but it becomes irrelevant if the war occurs in the next three to five years and all the F-22s deployed to the region are smoking ruins on destroyed air bases.

The US bomber fleet does not need to be in bases as close to where the action is likely to be as the fighter fleet does, because the bombers have much longer range and can attack targets in China from, for example, Diego Garcia in the Indian Ocean, or from bases in Australia. The US bombers, however, suffer from similar issues to the fighters, mainly lack of numbers and older fleets. In the type of war we are considering here, the bomber fleet is much more likely to use longer-range, standoff missiles, such as cruise missiles, than the traditional kinds of bombs that were flown over and dropped directly onto a target during World War II, Vietnam and even Iraq. This allows them to launch their missiles far from the target and outside the range of most air defences. Like other US air fleets, though, the bomber fleet is caught between older aircraft and new developments not yet available.

The US Air Force currently has 158 bombers in total, consisting of 62 B-1 Lancer bombers, 20 B-2 Spirit bombers, and 76 older B-52H Stratofortress bombers. It is the intention that the new B-21 will replace the 82 B-1 and B-2 bombers, while the B-52H will fly on through to at least the 2040s, if not into the 2050s, which would mean it will have seen 100 years of service by the time it is retired!

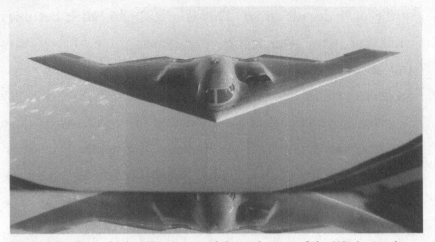

The B-2 Spirit stealth bomber is one of the mainstays of the US air attack force, along with B-1 Lancer bombers and older B-52H Stratofortress bombers. *(Getty)*

The US Air Force Assistant Chief of Staff for Plans and Programs, in written testimony to the House Armed Services Committee in 2021,[8] called for a fleet with only two bomber types within the 225 heavy bombers the US currently wants or thinks it can afford – still a substantial number. Subtracting the 76 older B-52 Stratofortress bombers, which are still effective but are to be used only as 'missile carriers', that leaves room within the desired fleet size of 225 for 149 B-21s. Apparently, because much of this is still secret, just five prototypes exist at the moment, and the first has not yet flown. The figure of 149 new B-21 bombers is nearly a 50% increase in demand for the B-21s by the US Air Force, up from its previous plans to buy only about 100 of the planes. By the 2050s, when the entire fleet of B-21s is likely to be operating, the total cost will be in the vicinity of $203 billion – not cheap and, as production occurs, they are likely to cost more than anticipated.

If that happens there will be a danger of 'sticker shock' – a negative response on the part of Congress and the administration in response to the final price, the sticker price, of each aircraft. This is always a risk with expensive military aircraft designs, except in countries like China where there is no public scrutiny. The usual result of sticker shock in the US is that the number of aircraft ordered is then cut back by the government as delivery approaches, with little consideration given to what might be needed based on the threat.

This is what happened with the B-2 during its public rollout in the late 1980s. Development of the aircraft began in 1981 and the procurement of 132 aircraft was approved in 1987. Yet it was only in April 1989 that the air force disclosed in public testimony that it had spent $22.4 billion on B-2 development. In early 1990, citing cost concerns and the end of the Cold War, Defense Secretary Dick Cheney cut the numbers of B-2s on order from 132 to 75. Later he trimmed that figure to just 20; Congress added one more later, resulting in the 21 planes eventually built. If we thought we needed 132 B-2s when the threat was Russia during the Cold War, I wonder how many the US might assess it needs in an honest appreciation of today's threat from China, even without Russia being in the equation.

DANGER ON OUR DOORSTEP

In peacetime, it is all about money. In wartime, and for the kind of war that China might fight against the US, it is all about the numbers. The total number of US aircraft does not come near the number of Chinese aircraft. And of course, China can concentrate all its aircraft in one area, the Western Pacific, but the US has worldwide responsibilities. Unfortunately for regional security, the situation regarding US aircraft numbers is unlikely to improve in the short to medium term, meaning China holds all the aces. This is something that should be at the front of Australians' minds if we are to contemplate joining the US in such a war.

The ability of China to protect its mainland bases from attack by US aircraft is also impressive. From the Chinese mainland, the effective, modern S-300 and S-400 surface-to-air missile systems China has bought from Russia, as well as China's domestic air-defence systems, have the range to reach out from China's mainland up to 400 kilometres, which means that these missile systems can shoot down any non-stealthy or less stealthy aircraft over Taiwan itself, which is only 180 kilometres off China's coast. To provide early warning, China has built multiple Over the Horizon-Backscatter (OTH-B) radars similar to the Australian Jindalee Operational Radar Network (JORN). This is a world-leading system in Australia which covers much of the Pacific to Australia's north, and there is no reason to believe that the Chinese version is any less capable.

It is said that when operational these Chinese radars will be able to detect and track even the very stealthy US B-2 and B-21 bombers.[9]

* * *

Fighters and their support aircraft are not the only forms of military power that either side is likely to deploy in a more traditional Taiwan war. It was always the US assumption that its navy would play a crucial role.

Comfortingly for Australia, because of our dependence on the US, the US Navy Secretary's new strategic guidance document, called *One Navy–Marine Corps Team* and released in 2021, makes it clear that the service now sees China as its number-one enemy, claiming that 'the long-term challenge posed by the People's Republic of China is the most significant for the Department. The People's Liberation Army Navy (PLAN) has radically expanded both its size and capabilities, growing to become the world's largest fleet.'[10] The document also promotes the US Navy Secretary's 'Four Cs' concept: China, Culture, Climate change and COVID, an acknowledgment that the US government has many urgent priorities competing for its restricted funds.

US maritime power across the world is based on its eleven carrier strike groups, its nine amphibious-ready groups and its nuclear-powered submarine force.

Aircraft carriers like the USS *Ronald Reagan* are the bedrock of the US Navy, allowing it to reach out and strike distant targets, including in the Western Pacific. *(Getty)*

The basis of the US Navy's ability to reach out and strike targets, the US carrier strike group consists of an aircraft carrier (often referred to as a 'supercarrier' because of its size compared to previous US aircraft carriers), with its 'air wing' of roughly 70 aircraft on each carrier; a number of cruisers, destroyers or frigates, all missile-armed; several supply ships; and often a nuclear submarine. There are perhaps 7500 crew in total across all ships in a carrier strike group.

An amphibious-ready group consists of navy ships that can carry US Marine Corps troops, equipment and aircraft to where they can conduct an amphibious assault. Aircraft in the group include the F-35B fighter; the MV-22 tiltrotor aircraft, capable of vertical take-off and landing and cruising at faster speeds like normal aircraft; and conventional attack and medium- and heavy-lift helicopters. An amphibious-ready group might be supported by a carrier strike group, as well as land-based aircraft if they are within range. These groups are 'task-organised', which means that they are assembled as needed to carry out any specific task. An amphibious-ready group normally carries about 5000 crew and troops.

To understand the limits of US naval power, it is important to realise that on any one peacetime day, only three of the eleven US carrier strike groups might be deployed: one each in the Pacific, the Atlantic and the Persian Gulf (although another one is currently being deployed in the Eastern Mediterranean because of the Ukraine War). Of the nine US amphibious-ready groups, four might be deployed: perhaps two in the Pacific, and one each in the Atlantic and the Gulf. The other carrier and amphibious groups are likely to be in rest, training or in maintenance at naval bases in Japan or on the US east and west coasts.

Massing forces takes time. During the Gulf War, it took six months to assemble overwhelming US and allied military power against a second-rate dictator. In a Taiwan war, China is not going to allow the US months.

During the Cold War era, the US Navy had confidence that, in a fleet-on-fleet engagement, its ships and carrier-based aircraft would be able to unleash missiles at a range beyond that of the Russian and Chinese navy's missiles. However, the Chinese have now caught up across the board, with near state-of-the-art systems on board many Chinese vessels that outrange the anti-ship weapons on US aircraft and ships.[11]

The US SM-6 missile – recently approved by Congress for sale to Australia – has a range of up to 370 kilometres from its launch ship and may work to remove some of this disadvantage for the US Navy if it can survive attacks by bigger ballistic missiles fired from the Chinese mainland. Yet the new Chinese anti-ship cruise missile YJ-18, with a range of up to 530 kilometres, would allow Chinese shooters to fire first because of the longer range: a significant advantage in modern maritime warfare, and one that for decades the US Navy thought it owned.

Fleet-on-fleet battles, in which a fleet of Chinese warships meets a fleet of US warships and they fight it out with the weapons they each have on board, may not take place early in such a war, or, if China strikes first with its mainland missiles and sinks a significant number of US ships, they may not happen at all. If fleet-on-fleet engagement does occur, considering the ability of China's missiles and rockets (with a range of 1500 to 3500 kilometres from the Chinese coast) to reach even the second island chain, China is likely to dominate.[12] As China specialists Toshi Yoshihara and

James R. Holmes write: 'Both the defensive and offensive sides of sea combat are stacking up in China's favour and progressively eroding or nullifying altogether some of the US Navy's tactical advantage.'[13]

The survivability of a US fleet, even in the second island chain, to say nothing of the first island chain, will be of critical importance to Australia. As mentioned, given the ties that have recently been refreshed through the AUKUS agreement, Australia is likely to be asked to send ships and aircraft to join an allied fleet. To do this, we must have some confidence that such a fleet can survive.

It would also be expected that the US submarine force would play a key role in any war with China, and the US seems to be preparing for that eventuality. The specific locations of the US Navy's submarines are unknown, but there was recently an exercise in the Pacific in which it was reported that 25 US submarines were active.[14] This was apparently an exercise in preparation for surging (sending out far more than the usual number) submarines into the Pacific if war with China eventuated.

It must be assumed, as previously discussed, that the US currently has nuclear-powered but not nuclear-armed submarines on patrol within the first island chain in the vicinity of Taiwan to act as a deterrent to a seaborne invasion. One class of nuclear subs is called the *Seawolf* class. There are only four of these submarines, as they proved too expensive to make, so a cheaper submarine, the *Virginia* class, was designed and is already in service. The *Seawolf*-class submarines carry at least 50 Tomahawk missiles, whose range can be in excess of 1000 kilometres. This class is faster, deeper diving and better armed than its *Los Angeles*–class predecessors and *Virginia*-class successors. To be effective, such submarines do not have to be actually in the Taiwan Strait, as their missiles have a very long reach. In July 2021, the US Navy deployed three of these exceptional submarines (USS *Seawolf*, *Connecticut* and *Jimmy Carter*) to the Pacific Ocean at the same time: an exceedingly rare occurrence.[15] It can only be assumed that this deployment was also a practice run for a surge of such submarines into the Pacific in response to a Taiwan war. But to surge anything, warning is required and why would China give warning?

The US Navy operates 69 nuclear-powered submarines. Fourteen carry nuclear-tipped ballistic missiles and are part of the US strategic nuclear force that deploys for very long patrols (months on end) and attempts to hide until they are needed to fire their missiles. Another four submarines of the 69 total are the *Seawolf* class, which are referred to as cruise missile submarines because that is their main weapon type. These cruise missiles were predominantly for stationary land targets but now have capability against ships at sea. This leaves 51 nuclear-powered attack submarines equipped with a variety of weapons that could be used against a Chinese fleet.

The US Navy may have 69 submarines at present but because US shipyards are not producing *Virginia*-class submarines as fast as other submarines are being retired, the navy's nuclear attack submarine fleet is smaller than is required now and is expected to be not greater than 50 submarines by 2026, despite the fact that the US Navy states that it needs 66 attack submarines. This may not be a problem the US Navy can overcome, because they are also short of ballistic missile submarines (the *Columbia* class) and are trying very hard to build more of these as well over the next 15 years in limited dockyards.

Under the 'Pivot to Asia' policy pursued by recent US administrations, 60% of US submarines are supposedly available to patrol the Pacific Ocean at any one time, which means roughly 31 attack submarines. The US can surge its submarine forces during a crisis, but normally one-third is on patrol, one-third is in training, and one-third is in maintenance. That deployment model is very common around the world and explains why the US Navy has just under 300 front-line ships but deploys only 100 at a time.[16] It means that the immediate availability of attack submarines in the Pacific might be as low as 10 or 11, with another 10 or 11 available after a surge period. As Yoshihara and Holmes assert, 'Twenty-two SSNs [nuclear-powered submarines], no matter how good they are individually, constitute a slender force to cover the vast China seas and the western Pacific in wartime.'[17] And unless fleet commanders can prepare for a surge – as the nation that initiates a surprise war can – increasing the number of submarines on patrol takes time.

So, as with aircraft, the US military faces a problem related to numbers. They do not have enough ships or submarines to match China, and they no longer have a technological edge over the Chinese navy. According to an article in *Defense One*:

> *The declining size of America's attack submarine fleet is particularly problematic given that the [Chinese] People's Liberation Army Navy fields more than 60 attack submarines. Admittedly, most of those submarines are diesel submarines. But China has at least seven SSNs and is working hard to increase both quality and quantity. To make matters worse, the United States must deploy its SSNs (attack submarines) around the world, whereas Beijing focuses almost all of its attack submarine deployments in the Indo-Pacific. That provides Beijing with a numerical advantage in attack submarines in locations where US–China conflict is most likely to occur.*[18]

RAND made the judgment in 2018 that US submarines pose a serious threat to China's navy and could possibly sink up to 40% of a Taiwan invasion fleet over a seven-day period in an engagement in the Taiwan Strait, but the report also observed that while this threat is still serious, it is decreasing.[19] China can now place devices on the sea floor to detect the presence of even the world's most sophisticated submarines, and its ability to destroy them is also growing. It is suspected that Russia has provided advanced nuclear depth-bomb technology to China, or China may have independently developed these bombs, as both the US and the UK have in the past. Regardless, it must be assumed that China has such weapons.

* * *

Can the US Navy increase its size and capability in the limited time that might be available to it? There is deep concern being expressed that the US Navy is not just too small, but also that it may not have a shipbuilding plan that would increase its size in place until 2023.

The US Navy is desperate not just to maintain its technological edge but also to regain the numbers it considers it needs to deter China. At the same time, it is examining every different idea that it has about how to actually fight with the fleet it has and be able to win. To illustrate how seriously the US is taking the need to integrate technology, fleet size and operational concept (how to fight), the US Chief of Naval Operations says:

> *The fleet plan will reflect various operational concepts that are being tested by the USN at present, such as Distributed Maritime Operations, Expeditionary Advanced Base Operations and Littoral Operations in a Contested Environment, as well as the results of the Large-Scale Exercise 21 wargame conducted in August 2021. The USN has also created a new operational unit TF 59 based in Bahrain to refine operational concepts.*[20]

Parts of these concepts have been exercised in the Philippines and recently in Australia, with the US Marines using a rocket system known as HIMARS, which Australia also hopes to possess sometime in the future. At this exercise, the Marines, with their HIMARS system, were deployed on Australian C-17 transport aircraft along with ground-protection elements, in the way such forces might be deployed into key positions in the first island chain.[21] So the US seems to be developing an operational concept similar to what is assumed to be China's new operational concept: to transport small groups armed with powerful anti-ship missiles very quickly by air onto islands along the first island chain, with or without the permission of the countries concerned, to be able to attack ships using the strait. This would either prevent the breakout of China's navy from the first island chain or assist the break-in of the US Navy from the second island chain. There would be no invasion or occupation of these territories; such techniques of troop deployment would simply be about locating small forces on these critical locations to act in concert with maritime or air forces.

Both China and the US are working on refining or radically changing how each will fight such a war. What this means is that both sides realise that the military equation has changed and both are trying to solve the new problem they face. In that respect, the question this book addresses is: as the situation changes due to the relative sizes of the forces and their technological competence, who will come to the right conclusion first?

Of course, these issues of tactics and numbers may already have been rendered irrelevant by the advantages conferred on the Chinese by the vast geography of the Pacific Ocean, the size of the PLA, the power of its rocket and missile force, and the vulnerability of both US bases and major US naval platforms such as aircraft carriers. None of the figures or tactics being planned over the long term will matter if, within a few years, China strikes first and is able to destroy US fleet units and bases with long-range missiles, block seaways and prevent America and its allies from reinforcing its Western Pacific units, and convince the likes of Japan, South Korea and Taiwan that there is no point in fighting on without US support. At that point, the big question for the US will be, should it respond with tactical nuclear weapons?

* * *

If China were successful in a sudden attack, as described in this book, it would then be essentially in control of the region, with little or no threat from the US. This is when the real test for Australia would begin, as we could be on our own for quite some time. Australia therefore has to plan not only for a sudden attack by China, but also what China might then do to Australia in the months or even years before the US could re-establish its power in the region.

A regionally dominant China represents an existential threat to Australia as a liberal democracy. It should be expected that, at the very least, China would demand access to Australia's resources at very favourable prices to overcome trade embargoes or to obtain cheap materials for its industries, even if it had also gained access to resources from other sources. China might even establish a military presence in this country, to guarantee access to resources and to stop the US using Australia as a military base for launching a counter-offensive. And a dominant China might just at some stage demand our agreement to the 14 demands made of us in 2020, and much more indeed.

The prospect of a war in the Western Pacific is dark enough for the US, but it is even darker for Australia, with our one-shot defence force, our enormous vulnerability as a nation if we or the US cannot control the seas over which we import products such as fuel, pharmaceuticals, fertiliser and hundreds of other critical items, and over which we export the natural resources that make us prosperous. The weakness of our once great and powerful ally will change just about every aspect of life in Australia. In the very short time that China might take to move from its peacetime routine to a wartime footing, Australia will not be able to make any substantial advancements to its military capability or its national resilience. So now is the time for Australia to act. Or have we already left it too late?

Can anyone imagine that if there was a widespread realisation that such a war faces us, more money for defence would not be found? But, as American General George C. Marshall said in 1942: 'The Army used to have all the time in the world and no money; now we've got all the money in the world and no time.'

A prudent Australia would have started to prepare 20 years ago. Accepting now that we have to make the most of things, we *must* start preparing for the right war now.

CHAPTER 12

AUSTRALIA, DEFEND YOURSELF!

If I have been asked once by my constituents, journalists or interested Australians I have been asked 100 times: if I had my way, what is the one thing that I would do for Australian national security? Just about everyone adds in their views before I can answer: B-21 bombers, F-22 fighters, conscription, reform of the Federation, nuclear weapons, a nuclear power industry ...

Apart from being able to go back in time and start again, there is no one solution to the problem of strengthening Australia's national security, but there are things that are more important than others. If I am forced by my interrogator to suggest a first step, my answer is always that it should be a comprehensive, formal strategy. If national security is truly the most important function of government, as I believe it is and as all governments claim it to be, then the government should initiate such a strategy, write the requirements for it and be closely involved in it.

Then, of course, there are many more steps that need to be taken before any Australian government can say that the nation is secure. The following, in priority order and greatly simplified, are the five steps I believe Australia needs to take to meet the demands of our current strategic environment.

1. Create a comprehensive national security strategy

The government should create a pro-active, medium- to long-term, comprehensive national security strategy, covering the nation's resilience as a whole and its defence, and making every cabinet minister aware of their national security responsibilities and holding them accountable. The classified version of the strategy must be brutally honest, but there must be an unclassified version that does not just engage the Australian people but also gives them confidence in a secure future. The objective of the strategy must be to maintain Australian sovereignty by making the nation self-reliant and resilient *in extremis*, and making the ADF more lethal and more sustainable and increasing its mass so that it really can, for as long as possible, deter war. Each of the descriptors I use to describe the nation and the ADF (self-reliant, resilient, lethal, sustainable and mass) have a very complex meaning themselves in this context, and must be judged against the kind of war (the threat) that the nation and the ADF could face over the next five to ten years, not against meaningless generalities as has been the case in the past. We must prepare for the right war.

As I have noted here and said often in interviews, the Australian Coalition government of 2013–22 has been the best government on national security that I have seen since the end of the Vietnam War. So, as a backbench senator, I was careful not to be too critical, and made a point of praising that government for having done so much in the sphere of defence. At the same time I continued to encourage and occasionally demand that the government did more to address the current geopolitical and military situation. And the more begins with a strategy.

Where Australia can do more is by, first, minimising the potential impact on Australia of the type of attack I have described in this book as a 'collateral attack' – that is, one that might be directed at Australia from within a war between China and the US. If we start to prepare for this eventuality, even if we cannot ultimately deter such an attack, we will at least be in a better position to mitigate its effects.

Second, our strategy must prepare Australia to survive a possible withdrawal of the US from the Western Pacific following a sudden successful Chinese attack on US bases in the worst case, and the temporary or permanent domination of the region by China.

The national security strategy that I advocate should give broad guidance to ministers and may require the preparation by every minister, not just the traditional national security ministers, of nested national security strategies, for approval by the National Security Committee of Cabinet.[1] By nested, I mean that a national security strategy is the overarching strategy, and defence, energy, social and industry strategies, plus many others, fit neatly into it.

Some of the outcomes of a government strategy process were dealt with by the then Prime Minister in two recent speeches. The first was on 1 July 2020 in respect of what the Department of Defence called a Strategic Update, which explained how an extra $270 million provided by the government to Defence would be spent. The Prime Minister's defence-related speech was much broader than just defence, which contributed to the confusion in Australian minds that national security is something that Defence does.

The reason that Australia needs such a strategy now when, supposedly, we have not needed it in the past is because of what Prime Minister Morrison referred to as 'hybrid warfare'. Hybrid warfare as a theory of *military* strategy has traditionally referred to a blending of various forms of warfare into a hybrid: political, conventional, irregular and cyber warfare to give a few examples. Prime Minister Morrison described 'hybrid warfare' as conflict that has 'stripped away the old boundaries that once separated the realms of defence, foreign policy, trade and investment, communications and other areas, reaching deep into our domestic society'.[2] This is an acceptable definition of what Australian strategy needs to face and this awareness compares favourably in my view to the ad-hoc way that Australian governments have approached strategy up until now, essentially by taking one problem or issue at a time and solving it. While this has worked in the past, we now need a much more comprehensive approach. And although the Coalition government dealt successfully with individual national security problems that arose, Australia still lags seriously behind the changes in our strategic environment that now demand a comprehensive approach.

At the risk of losing the attention of every strategy purist but recognising the reality of politics, it matters less what such a strategy is called than that the problem of national security is considered as a single issue, driven by government, covering both defence and the nation in its entirety. The end product of the process is not the written strategy, but national security itself. We must be secure, so a strategy must be produced, reviewed and implemented. Looking at the experiences of other countries (the US, the UK and India, for example), a national security strategy is unlikely to be completed successfully in the first review cycle; it may take a few years and a few attempts (which is why I have been advocating for this for at least a decade!).

But the process itself will produce benefits for ministers, for bureaucrats and for national leaders.

My observation as a humble backbencher is that Australian ministers do not like this process. They would rather be left to themselves to work out, in their own time, what they need to do to achieve what they think is necessary for national security. This approach might work during the kind of peace that Australia has enjoyed for the last 75 years, but it will not work as we move into a less stable period when we need to produce results across all aspects of the nation and government, and to produce them quickly.

I have also observed that the idea of producing a *written* national security strategy is not popular with Coalition leaders, who prefer some government policy to remain much more informal. I suspect that is because the only experience most of our leaders have of a national security strategy is the one produced by the Labor government in 2013. This was not a true national security strategy, in that it did not cover all government functions, nor did it allocate responsibilities or have an accountability process. It achieved little except consume the bureaucracy for a period of time at the end of a very difficult period of government. The national security strategy that I advocate does not have to be like the previous Labor Party version. But, given the crisis-like situation that Australia finds itself in as regards security in our region, with danger on our doorstep, strong direction is required, objectives must be set, coordination is needed across government, and accountability is essential.

2. Continue addressing legacy problems with national security

The government should continue to address legacy national security issues, such as the need for specific legislation to empower security bodies such as the Australian Security and Intelligence Organisation (ASIO) and the Australian Federal Police, steps to counter foreign influence, and deficiencies in skills enhancement, naval shipbuilding, anti-terrorism procedures, cyber technology, modern industry, liquid fuels, intelligence and policing, biosecurity (pandemics), universities, health and, the basis of national security, the economy. Recently, the former government's Minister for Defence and Defence Industry Minister addressed some enduring problems and produced solid results, but in the area of national security, of which Defence is only part, it is very hard to achieve quick results. Yet quick results are what is needed.

I do not advocate that the government should stop projects or development so that the bureaucracy can conduct a long and detailed 'white-paper approach' to national security. This has been the practice for years – when a white paper–type review is announced, just about everything in defence stops to await its completion, often for years.

Australia cannot afford that this time. The government should decide what needs to be done and do it. It must not leave these issues to be addressed by the bureaucracy.

3. Develop plans to fight the China war

The government, being strategic, at some stage must formulate actual plans for how a China war can be fought. The first step in doing this, if it is not already occurring at a classified level, is to insist on a seat at US warfighting strategy or planning tables – that is, wherever the US is making its strategic and operational plans, in Washington at the Pentagon or in Hawaii, the headquarters of Indo-Pacific Command. Only by getting across an appropriate degree of detail about how a war between the US and China will be fought can Australia consider what role it might play in that war. It is a waste of time for Australia to be trying to work out how we will contribute to US efforts by readying and deploying a group of ships and aircraft to the Western Pacific if the initial stages of the war are likely to be over before our ships clear the heads in Sydney Harbour, or our aircraft, which need US tanker support to deploy from Australia to Japan or Guam, find that the tankers have already been destroyed. These are the discussions that should be occurring now, not the day after a sudden attack.

It is never too early to start such planning, given the critical nature of this war for the US, Australia and our region. Only by looking in detail at US expectations of its allies, which will not become firm until the military planning begins, will Australia become aware of how the US assesses the risks, what the US needs from Australia, and what Australia can provide. The government must come to terms with the lack of confidence within the US in relation to this war and assess whether it is winnable before we commit. Australia will be a junior partner in this war, but that does not mean that it cannot influence US strategy at the highest level. Not only can we, but we *must* have a voice in strategy and in military operations.

There are any number of operational issues related to strategy that must be clarified with the US before Australia commits military forces. How does the US see this war going: nuclear or conventional? Will it have a slow build-up of tension or be a surprise attack? When might it occur? Will Taiwan and US bases be attacked simultaneously, or just Taiwan initially? What would a coalition expect of Japan, South Korea and India? Only once we have agreed with the US on such issues can a feasible military strategy emerge.

History tells us that leaders of coalitions or alliances sometimes have quite unreasonable expectations of junior allies. Churchill certainly had an unreasonable expectation of Australia once the Japanese had attacked Pearl Harbor and Singapore and were bombing Darwin. He requested that Australia's only battle-ready and experienced army divisions, which at that point were aboard ships on the way from North Africa to defend Australia, be diverted to Burma, because that was his priority. The Australian government split the difference, bringing most troops home but leaving some in Ceylon (present-day Sri Lanka).

4. Prepare for enhanced grey-zone conflict

Australia is handling the current level of China's grey-zone conflict well, with measures that lessen our trade dependency, strengthen cyber defence and attack, stop the theft of intellectual property, and recognise the link between national security and the economy and the need to defend our political systems and our institutions. The new national security strategy I propose is likely to indicate that Australia must prepare for an enhanced grey-zone conflict that is still short of war. This may require the government to

- prepare for more lethal and unattributable biological attacks, cyber-attacks and attacks on satellites
- be prepared for further anti-trade measures that might be deployed against Australia, such as threats that discourage or stop companies from shipping to and from Australia, or make foreign shipping prohibitively expensive by dramatically increasing insurance rates

- increase Australia's liquid-energy resilience by increasing our production of crude oil, our domestic refining capacity, our storage of crude oil and refined petroleum products, and our ability to move crude oil by ship, rail or pipeline from source to refinery, which may involve the purchase of some oil tankers and rail rolling stock, and the construction of storage facilities
- encourage Australian companies that are important for national security through policies that reward a physical presence in Australia, rather than judging companies on their competitive advantage and 'value for money', as with many current government policies
- create and protect systems and processes (not the actual implementation at this stage) for the mobilisation of the nation's resources that would be needed if the grey-zone conflict developed into physical conflict – in essence get the systems ready in this phase for what might have to be done to mobilise the nation at a later time
- set up an organisation that can, when necessary, direct personnel, skills and resources across the nation to warlike needs
- support regional neighbours and allies against attempts to woo them away from Australian

influence or reduce the effectiveness of alliances, especially in the South Pacific.

The above measures would also be applicable to wartime and would significantly increase the self-reliance and resilience of the nation. The government would be very wise during this period to demand access to our allies' contingent strategies and operations, similar to the arrangements between NATO member states during the Cold War.

5. Fund defence according to need

Australia should never forget that diplomacy and alliances are our first line of defence. Australia has a fine diplomatic record and has built a network of alliances and is now working to improve them. We need to ensure, however, that our hard economic and military power matches our diplomatic clout, which in turn would make us a much more valuable alliance partner.

Australia's defence capability should not be defined by our materiel, by the amount we spend on defence, or by government or bureaucratic spin. Our deteriorating strategic environment now demands that our national security be defined by what the nation and the ADF can actually do to deter or to win a future war with China. The emphasis in defence, and in government statements about defence, must change from concentrating on dollars and percentage of GDP spent, and on the purchase of submarines, ships, planes and tanks, to determining the kind of war that the defence force, backed by a resilient and self-reliant nation, can resolve in Australia's favour. This involves aligning strategy, operational concepts and the military equipment the nation is buying, but always begins with a definition of the threat.

Stemming from the analysis in this book, the following, although not an exhaustive list, might be seen as government priorities in this area:

- establishing a ballistic missile defence of key points in Australia
- accelerating the development of Australia's lethal longer-range strike capability, which should cover at least the Indonesian Archipelago and the South Pacific, and commence the development, over a sustained period, of a strike capability that can reach even further
- increasing our ability to keep key Australian ports open while under threat from modern sea mines
- ensuring that the essential needs of the nation can be provided domestically for a realistic period in the absence of commercial sea transport, which may require setting aside the previous Coalition government's attachment to liberal ideologies of

'value for money' and 'the pre-eminences of the market'

- ensuring all existing weapons systems can be operated at maximum combat rates for extended periods, backed up by adequate manpower and logistics – the essence of modern mobilisation and sustained warfighting
- hardening key air bases to increase their survivability against strikes by the full range of China's weapons – especially if critical US aircraft are going to be stationed on our bases – and preparing for the quick dispersion of vulnerable assets as protection against surprise attack
- increasing our ability to move a limited amount of shipping around the coast of Australia for transportation of key bulk commodities and justifying the current and future construction of inland railways on national security grounds
- understanding, in the context of deciding the size, timing and type of our support for a contribution to a regional alliance, how disastrous it would be for homeland defence if Australia deployed our best warfighting forces from our one-shot ADF to support the US in the Western Pacific and they suffered severe casualties, and China subsequently became the dominant power in our region

- ensuring that the ADF can function logistically, in terms of liquid fuel, weapons, missiles, spare parts etc, at combat rates, for an extended period of time (six months or a year) if Australia is denied access to commercial sea or air transport
- planning to increase the size of the ADF (in the first instance aircraft, including drones, and warships) in accordance with the conclusions of the national security strategy, by procurement or by retaining assets that would in the past have been retired when new materiel was introduced, to match the tasks the ADF must conduct concurrently and to make the ADF less of a one-shot force
- significantly increasing the voluntary reserve element in each service, to increase mass and sustainability and to help Australians recognise that defence is the responsibility of the whole nation
- acknowledging, with a view to gaining public support, that the cost of defending our nation should no longer be based on what a government thinks it can afford, but on what the strategic environment demands.

* * *

The time for complacency for Australians is over, and now the task is to build real strength. While those engaged in strategic and military policy are fond of talking about an 'uncertain strategic environment', we now have a better understanding than ever of our potential strategic threats. China – either in concert with others or alone – is capable of challenging the US, dominating the Western Pacific and harming Australia's interests to the extent that Australia as a liberal democracy is in danger, so preparing for a China war must be the standard we judge ourselves by. And we have a good idea of the strategic objectives that China might fight for: promoting the CCP's leadership by diminishing US power and retrieving the 'renegade province' of Taiwan.

China's recent actions in the South China Sea, its use of trade embargoes and cyber-attacks, and its increasingly authoritarian leadership mean that we are already in a conflict that does not yet involve violence. In the leadup to a war, China will use the grey-zone tactics we are currently experiencing in stronger and more potent ways. If it does proceed to war, it will likely have the strategic advantage of being the 'first mover', using the greatest military weapons in world history: deception and surprise. There is no saying how long we have before it exercises this advantage.

In the face of China's aggression, Australian governments must continue to lead decisively on national security, and the Australian people must support moves to protect national sovereignty and promote resilience. This requires action on many fronts, especially using diplomacy to encourage US strength and deter China's adventurism. It must also include strengthening our economy so it can absorb the shock of conflict and, most importantly, making the ADF larger, more potent and more capable of fighting for an extended period.

Only a complete package, as the result of a national security strategy that creates self-reliance and resilience, will give Australia a real chance of deterring the conflict that we do not want. War is a terrible thing. But the only thing that is worse is being involved in a war and losing.

A NEW REALITY

The world still turns the day after the satellites tumble from the sky, and it will keep on turning. Empires come and go in world history and the gods that insignificant humans invented to explain the world look down and shake their heads. With the Chinese attack in the Pacific, another empire, the US 'empire', has been challenged for primacy on the third rock from the sun.

For the gods this is hardly noteworthy. Every previous empire, dynasty or caliphate, whether it be the Abbasid, the Portuguese, the Spanish, the Qing, the Mongol, the Russian, the Roman or the British, thought it would last forever, and their leaders and people began to take that eternal existence for granted. But they were not special and they did not last.

The wonderfully inventive human brain, which has brought so much good to the world, seems incapable of avoiding the pitfall of complacency. The British philosopher

Thomas Hobbes, living in the early stages of the British Empire, described the life of man as 'solitary, poor, nasty, brutish and short' and so in many ways set the objectives of what good nations should strive to improve. Of all the nations on the face of the Earth through world history, few have made greater progress in overcoming, for the good of its citizens, the five characteristics of Hobbes's world. Few have come as close to perfection as Australia. But now Australians have to understand how and why their world is being challenged.

Since Hobbes's time, both good and evil have marked the progress of the world through empires, and Australians must remember that wars come and go, that it was only 80 years ago that Italian, German and Japanese fascism, totalitarianism and militarism was defeated by our parents or grandparents – just as an elderly Ukrainian woman looking into a TV camera in a ruined street reminds us that she has seen war before and wonders why Russian President Putin does not just go home.

In the absence of the ever-demanding hum of servers and computers in a world cut off from its accustomed means of communications by the rise of yet another empire seeking primacy at the expense of its neighbours, Australians are perhaps contemplating that there is evil in the world, and what the world democracies have created for the betterment of man can only in the end be sustained by vigilance and by strength.

But philosophy is the last thing on the minds of Australia's citizens and their leaders on the days after the sudden and vicious attack by China. Most people are merely aware that the world had changed forever. The post–World War II era is over. The mighty United States of America, whose physical presence and power has facilitated security and prosperity, has suffered a defeat far worse and far more sudden than any in its history. The most powerful of its military organisations, the Indo-Pacific Command, has been smashed, and tens of thousands of its members have been killed or injured. The likelihood of the US being able to fight back in the short to medium term is very much an unknown.

China has made its move and that move has been almost totally successful because of the complacency of the world towards the potential malice of an authoritarian power. Few thought that Russia would move on one of its European neighbours, yet it did. And few applied the lessons of Ukraine to other parts of the world. After one authoritarian nation under its brutal dictator mounted a war of aggression in a supposedly 'civilised' part of the world, there was no reason why another equally brutal dictator would not do the same in our part of the world. The bravery of the Ukrainians in fighting the Russians, the surprising incompetence of the Russian military, the willingness of the world to apply sanctions against

Russia and to supply weapons to Ukraine meant that Russia encountered far greater resistance than it expected. Could these lessons not be transferred from Russia to China? Might not China draw a completely different set of lessons from Russia's experience in Ukraine? Would it take advantage while the attention of the democracies was fixed on Ukraine? Was Sino arrogance so marked that they believed they would never make the errors that Russia had made?

Not only has China smashed the US military in the Western Pacific, it has almost totally prevented the return of US forces by securing the first and second island chains and removing any bases that the US might have relied on to support its future moves. China has sent small groups of troops with missiles to every strait in the first island chain without the permission of any of the countries involved. Backed up by its intact air force and navy, it is able to prevent any US ship from entering the first island chain and approaching the Chinese mainland or Taiwan, and using judiciously positioned commercial ships, it has blocked the Suez and Panama canals to slow the redeployment of US and allied forces, if in fact they try to move from Europe or other places to the Pacific. China has even located small forces in Papua New Guinea and one area of the South Pacific, the Solomon Islands, to allow it to monitor Australia and prevent it being used as a base for US forces.

China is now the only nation in the world which still has fully functioning space operations and cyber systems. It is willing to permit others to re-open their communications to a limited extent but only as far as it suits China's needs, for instance to communicate with China or to spread concern and confusion. For the time being, President Xi is happy to let the rest of the world stew in its fears about this new, uncertain world.

* * *

The impact of the attack on Australia's military and infrastructure is enormous. Australian governments and agencies learn very quickly of the substantial damage to our modern and expensive air force, which were left vulnerable, with planes sitting on open tarmac or inside hangars designed to keep off the weather but not cruise missiles fired from submarines. The Australian navy tries twice to move ships from inner harbour mooring points, once in Sydney Harbour itself and once at its Fleet Base West near Perth, and both ships are struck by mines inserted by Chinese submarines from outside the harbour in the days following the attack on the air force bases. From then on not a single navy ship can move until the slow process of clearing the harbour of mines is completed. Only one harbour at a time can be cleared because the navy does not have the resources to do more. Ships that were at sea at the time of the attack *are ordered to stay at sea until the safe use of the harbours can be guaranteed.*

Some Australian officials have experience of crisis management, having recently dealt with drought, floods, pandemics and widespread fires, but no Australian government has faced a situation like the current one since 1941 and there is absolutely no national memory. The so called 'War Book', a guide to what should happen in a defence emergency, has not been reviewed for decades. It's still an actual book, a hard copy so out of date and so full of generalisations from another era as to be of no use at all. And of course, the days after the massive attack on our major ally and a significant attack on this country do not lend themselves to the calm study of historic documents. The federal government knows enough to adopt the total emergency defence powers that are clearly in the constitution and which enable the federal government to take any action that it sees fit, but of course with most of the normal communications still down, and without a clear picture of what is happening overseas, and without a tradition of strategy-making itself and with no preparation for such an event, what action needs to be taken by the federal government and with what priority is unclear. The big question as the weeks go by is whether there will be another Chinese attack, either on the US or on Australia. Is this the end of the violence or only the beginning?

The most immediate needs of the population are the most pressing, regardless of what happens overseas, or whether there is another attack or not. People need food and transport, and they need leadership.

For a period of days, what is on the supermarket shelves on the day of the attack will be all there is for some time. Recalling the panic buying that occurred during the early days of the COVID pandemic, shoppers rush to the supermarkets, though many shops remain closed since the attack. Australia is never going to be short of food, but it is certainly going to be some time before it can be moved from fields to factories and then to markets, given that Australia is dependent on diesel truck transport, roads and supermarkets. Australia had less than 30 days of liquid fuel (diesel, petrol and aviation fuel) in the country at the time of the attack. Successive governments spoke of having twice that number of days of fuel because another 30 days' worth was always on its way in tankers. But after the attack not one commercial oil tanker docks at an Australian port, due to fear of mines in ports and a belief that insurance will not cover acts of war. Even tankers close to Australian ports turn about and go back to a safe harbour at the direction of their owners or on their captain's initiative. The remaining two refineries in Australia are commissioned to increase production to the maximum, but they were already working at 90% capacity to produce only 10% of Australia's needs.

There is no spare capacity. States are directed to permit the exploitation of crude oil still in the ground or just offshore, but this will take months at least, and Australia will have no refined fuel in less than 30 days. The government has no answer because it assumed it would never have to face this problem. It relied on a strategy of hope.

The governments' priorities become food, fuel and governance (law and order). Backed by its defence emergency powers, the federal government is able to act relatively decisively in regard to directing state governments and other agencies. It is not prepared to establish a war cabinet including the opposition so early in this emergency, but it makes attempts to consult with the opposition parties. Leadership itself is difficult. Although most of the domestic mass-communications channels are re-established within days, without international news feeds that give context to what a prime minister is expected to say in these circumstances, it is hard for the head of government to speak authoritatively, and what news there is, mostly isn't good.

Limited communications with the world are restored as permitted by China but Australia has no backup satellites to relaunch despite the obvious need for them, and the sea cables will take years to repair.

As time goes on, Australian standards of living collapse. Without petrol or diesel, many people cannot get to their places of employment. While many can work from home using the internet where the internet has been restored, the need for such service workers diminishes. People need physical goods, produced by workers in factories or on farms, that you can either eat or put into a vehicle, not lifestyle services.

Health services take some time to collapse, as the reserves of most pharmaceuticals last for up to six months. But because spare parts for the nation's generators of base load power come from overseas, the supply of electricity to the cities and the little industry Australia has becomes unreliable. The lights across the nation do not go out, as solar power and hydro power keep some of them on, but the extraordinary lifestyle Australians have enjoyed is only a dim memory.

Key cargo is flown in on commercial cargo aircraft, which have all been requisitioned by the government for this purpose. But how can you find the critical spare parts for a modern society from overseas when the coordination of the internet is missing? How can you send a cargo aircraft to the right place in North America or Europe to find the right item? And what will happen when there is no aviation fuel?

* * *

Diplomacy, deprived of modern communications, cannot achieve very much quickly. Governments are used to having instantaneous control over ambassadors due to very fast communications, and leaders had been able to speak directly to each other in ways unknown before in history. Communications have been limited yet the need to communicate has never been more important.

When President Xi feels ready, China's post-attack diplomacy begins. It enters negotiations with Japan and South Korea first, then Taiwan, then the US, then Southeast Asia and, finally, Australia. China has achieved its aims with almost no damage to its cities, its industries, its people or its military, and now it has every desire to secure its strategic objectives of removing the US from the Western Pacific and reincorporating Taiwan without the use of force.

China's message is now one of reasonableness, peace, growth and stability. It only wants good things for all the countries in the region, it maintains, now that the US is gone. And not only good for the region but for the world. China needs to trade with the world to maintain its own internal social cohesion, but on this occasion it had put its strategic objectives ahead of trade for the short term. Now it is back to playing the long game, one backed by overwhelming military force.

It promises Japan and South Korea that if they accept the new regional power situation, then China will forego any territorial claims it may have against either country and will respect the sovereignty of both. The quicker both countries accept the new situation, the sooner trade and normality will recommence. Then, says China, with the US out of the region, Asia will once again be for Asians.

The message to the US is blunt. You are out of the Western Pacific and we will not let you re-establish your bases in Japan, South Korea or even Guam. From Japan to Australia and out to Hawaii, the Western Pacific is now a Chinese sphere of influence. The US's regional allies are not going to fight on without the US, so the US must accept the new situation. Even Taiwan will now willingly joint the PRC.

To Taiwan, the message is even more blunt. Now is the time to think of where your future best lies, the Chinese diplomats say, as an autonomous province of the PRC, your home. If you now willingly join the PRC, you will continue to enjoy prosperity and security and China combined with Taiwan will be a global powerhouse. The alternative is too awful to contemplate. If Taiwan does not accept reincorporation, China will achieve it by force. Japan and South Korea will not fight and, without the US, Taiwan will be defenceless. Your autonomy will be guaranteed under the conditions of your reincorporation, say the diplomats. Come willingly.

The message to Australia is also threatening. China had assessed that if they were successful with the sudden attack, the only way for the US to re-establish military power in the region would be by projecting power from Hawaii, Alaska, the west coast of the US and from Australia. There was nothing that China could do about preventing US power being assembled in US territories (except for Guam and other mid-ocean territories), but it is determined that Australia will not be used as a base for a US counter-offensive against China. US forces must not be permitted under any circumstances to use Australia as a base. If Australia allows this, or any other action that supports US influence in the Western Pacific, the South Pacific or the Indian Ocean, then China will be obliged to take direct action against Australia, which might involve sanctions, blockade and even occupation.

China tells Australia that it regrets it had to act against the Australian military and is sorry for the loss of life. But Australia must now recognise that its region has changed and if Australia wants to maintain any shred of sovereignty, if it wants to open its sea routes to commercial shipping and import and export goods, then it has to reject any involvement with the US military. In effect, Australia must become a tributary state of China.

Australia has lost its air force and the ability to use its navy and its ports, its army is irrelevant and it has no sovereignty now except as permitted by China. Australia faces an enormous decision – does Australia accept China's direction and do what it has been told in relation to the US, or does it defy China and stand beside the US, impotent though both countries are, with the awful consequences that might entail?

As time goes on, the anarchist part of Australian society takes to demonstrating on the streets. Riots at food distribution points become frequent and cannot be controlled by normal policing methods. The worst in Australia's fringe society comes to the fore. Australian society is no different from any other society in relation to the observance of law and order. Even during natural disasters, the mateship that Australians talk about so often has strong elements of myth about it. Of course, some people help others and show bravery, but others steal and loot their neighbours' properties. On occasions, law and order have to be enforced with draconian methods. This is our brave new world.

Australian society is as fragile as any other society in the world and that this would surprise many Australians is only because our society has been spared for so long the effects of the worst kind of unnatural disaster – war. The dominant thought in most Australian minds by this point is that anything that is required to restore normalcy as it has been understood since 1945 should be done. There is enormous pressure on the government to take Australia and Australians back to the so recent past. Against the practicality of day-to-day living, as the economy and society collapse, the notion of liberal democracy, by now only defendable through a war against China, is a difficult idea to sell.

And what in reality can Australia do? Its greatest ally is licking its wounds. Its neighbours have rolled over and accepted China as the regional hegemon. Its greatest adversary has re-presented the grievances that it dumped on Australia back in 2020: accept Huawei; remove foreign interference laws; forget about the origins of COVID; permit no US forces to use Australian bases; refrain from criticising China on the South China Sea, human rights and cyber-attacks; join the Belt and Road Initiative; and finally, re-price (downwards and severely) your exports of coal and iron ore to China.

The Australian government looks seriously at these demands. Because that is what happens to tributary states.

ENDNOTES

Prologue: Out of the Blue?

1 Commonwealth, *Parliamentary Debates*, House of Representatives, 6 July 1950, p. 3 (Robert Menzies, Prime Minister).

Chapter 1: Rise to Power

1 Davidson, P., 'Statement of Admiral Philip S. Davidson, U.S. Navy Commander U.S. Indo-Pacific Command before the House Armed Services Committee on U.S. Indo-Pacific command posture 10 March 2021', pp. 31–40.

2 Medcalf, R., *Contest for the Indo-Pacific*, La Trobe University Press, Melbourne, 2020, pp. 46–48, 221, 265.

3 Medcalf, *op. cit.*, pp. 30 and 372–3.

4 Hayton, B., *The Invention of China*, Yale University Press, New Haven, Connecticut, 2020, p. 352. See also Garnaut, J., 'National Socialism with Chinese characteristics', *Foreign Policy*, 15 November 2012.

5 Hayton, *op. cit.*, p. 352.

6 McCann, D., 'National Socialism with Chinese Characteristics', *Spectator Australia*, 21 February 2021.

7 Hayton, *op. cit.*, pp. 350–2. Also McCann, *op. cit.*

8 Mastro, O.S., 'How China is bending the rules in the South China Sea', *The Interpreter*, Lowy Institute, 10 February 2021;

283

Maizland, L., 'China's repression of Uyghurs in Xinjiang', *Council on Foreign Relations*, 1 March 2021.

Chapter 3: Wolf Warriors

1 Kelly, P., 'Australia has shown great resilience in the face of China's aggression', *The Australian*, 10 July 2021.
2 Lema, K., 'Philippines defence chief says was urged by China to drop review of U.S. pact', *Reuters*, 30 September 2021.
3 For example, see Brand, H., 'China is a declining power – and that's the problem', *Foreign Policy*, 24 September 2021; and Patey, L., 'China is an economic bully – and weaker than it looks', *Foreign Policy*, 4 January 2021.
4 Beckley, M., and Brands, H., 'The end of China's rise', *Foreign Affairs*, 1 October 2021.
5 Beckley, M., *Unrivaled: Why America Will Remain the World's Sole Superpower*, Cornell University Press, Ithaca, 2018.
6 Ellis, S., 'Taiwan remains China's fatal attraction', *Australian Financial Review*, 8 March 2022.
7 Mead, W.R., 'Xi Jinping's two-track foreign policy', *Wall Street Journal*, 11 October 2021.
8 *Ibid.*
9 Talbot, J., 'CCP sanctioned video threatens China will nuke Japan in a "full-scale war"', *Sky News*, 19 July 2021.

Chapter 4: In the Grey Zone

1 Hanson, F., Currey, E. and Beattie, T., 'The Chinese Communist Party's coercive diplomacy', *Australian Strategic Policy Institute*, Canberra, 2020, pp. 4–5.
2 Sanger, D., *The Perfect Weapon: War, Sabotage, and Fear in the Cyber Age*, Scribe Publications, Melbourne, 2018.
3 Sanger, *op. cit.*, pp. 118–130.
4 Morrison, S., 'Morrison's messages to the "sophisticated state-based cyber actor"', *Lowy Institute*, 19 June 2020.

5   Lowy Institute Poll, comparing results for 2006 with 2021; see: https://poll.lowyinstitute.org/charts/threats-australias-vital-interests.

6   Gertz, B., 'Chinese military seeks to dominate from space, deploys war-fighting tools into orbit', *Washington Times*, 13 October 2021.

7   Brown, L., 'Military chiefs warn of space bullying by Russia and China', *The Australian*, 30 July 2021.

8   Wigston, Air Chief Marshal M., UK Space Command, www.facebook.com/royalairforce/videos/uk-space-command-the-chief-of-the-air-staff-air-chief-marshal-sir-mike-wigston-o/896042440948263/.

9   Brown, *op. cit.*

10 Tidsall, S., 'Little blue men: The maritime militias pushing China's claims', *The Guardian*, 16 May 2016.

Chapter 5: Where and When?

1   While there is no single 'official' government scenario, there is significant speculation in Australia about the possibility of conflict over Taiwan and its implications for Australia. For examples, see: Grieber J., Smith, M. and Tillet, A., 'Canberra prepares for Taiwan conflict as tensions escalate', *Australian Financial Review*, 16 April 2021; Medcalf, *op. cit.*, p. 373; Roggeveen, S., 'Will ANZUS make it to 80?', *The Interpreter*, Lowy Institute, 1 September 2021; and Burshtein, D., 'The Taiwan tango: a delicate dance for Australia', *Spectator Australia*, 4 February 2021.

2   Funaiole, M.P. and Glaser, B.S., 'China's provocations around Taiwan aren't a crisis', *Center for Strategic and International Studies*, 19 May 2020.

3   Tsirbas, M., 'What does the nine-dash line actually mean?', *The Diplomat*, 2 June 2016.

4   Yoshihara, T. and Holmes, J. R., *Red Star over the Pacific: China's Rise and the Challenge to U.S. Maritime Strategy*, second edition, Naval Institute Press, Annapolis, 2018, p. 73.

5   Moseley, T.M. and Corley, J.D.W., 'The next DC tanker battle could determine who wins the next war', *RealClear Defense*, 7 October 2021; Holmes, J., 'Defend the first island chain', *Proceedings*, April 2014.

6   Missile Defense Project, 'Missiles of China', *Missile Threat: Center for Strategic and International Studies*, 14 June 2018; see also Shugart, T., 'Australia and the growing reach of China's military', *Lowy Institute Analyses*, 9 August 2021.

7   'Chinese air force video shows major H-6 bomber strike on Guam-resembling island', *Military Watch*, 22 September 2020.

8   Ellis, S., 'As fears of a PLA invasion grow, analysts offer possible scenarios', *Taipei Times*, 11 October 2020.

9   China Power Team, 'How is China modernizing its nuclear forces?', *ChinaPower: Center for Strategic and International Studies*, 10 December 2019.

10 'Taiwan defence minister pushes new arms spending, says China tensions worst in four decades', *Reuters*, 6 October 2021.

11 Robinson, L., *Tell Me How This Ends: General David Petraeus and the Search for a Way Out of Iraq*, PublicAffairs, New York, 2008.

Chapter 6: The Response: the US and Its Allies

1   Copp, T., '"It failed miserably": After wargaming loss, joint chiefs are overhauling how the US military will fight', *Defense One*, 6 July 2021.

2   Ullman, H., 'America's flawed war strategies', *The Hill*, 15 June 2021; Mattis, J., 'Summary of the 2018 National Defense Strategy of the United States of America', US Department of Defense, 2018, p. 6.

3   *A National Security Strategy for a New Century*, The White House, October 1998, p. 7.

4   Congressional Budget Office, *Illustrative Options for National Defense under a Smaller Defense Budget*, October 2021.

5   Cordesman, A.H. and Hwang, G., 'The Biden administration: Strategy and reshaping the national security budget', *Center for Strategic and International Studies*, 16 February 2021.

6   Feldscher, J., 'CIA creates China center to shift to great power competition', *Defense One*, 8 October 2021.

7   Spoehr, T., Bowman, B., Clark, B. and Eaglen, M., 'What to expect when you're expecting a National Defense Strategy', *War on the Rocks*, 27 September 2021.

8   Townshend, A., Thomas-Noone, B. and Steward, M., 'Averting crisis: American strategy, military spending and collective defence in the Indo-Pacific', *United States Studies Centre*, University of Sydney, 19 August 2019.

9   Gould, J., 'Debate on "no first use" of nukes mushrooms in Washington', *Defense News*, 7 October 2021.

10 *Ibid.*

11 Spoehr, Bowman, Clark and Eaglen, *op. cit.*

12 *Ibid.*

13 Mehta, A., 'Inside US Indo-Pacific command's $20 billion wish list to deter China – and why Congress may approve it', *Defense News*, 2 April 2020.

14 'Senator Hawley continues to stand with Taiwan, introducing new bill to help nation arm itself', *Josh Hawley, US Senator for Missouri*, 21 November 2021, quoted in Abodo, S., 'Congress must pass Senator Hawley's Arm Taiwan Act', *Newsweek*, 11 November 2021.

15 Abodo, *op. cit.*

Chapter 7: The Response: Australia

1   Church, N., 'The Australia–United States defence alliance', *Parliament of Australia*.

2   Dibb, P., 'Radical new defence policy or Hill's smoke and mirrors?', *The Australian*, 16 December 2005, cited in 'Australia's national security: A defence update 2003, 2005 and 2007', *Parliament of Australia*.

3 Department of Foreign Affairs and Trade, 'Trade and investment at a Glance 2019', Australian Government, 2019.

4 Dale, T., 'The G20: A quick guide', *Parliament of Australia*, 4 March 2014.

5 For examples of China's emphasis on readiness and the use of force, see Lie Zhen, 'Xi Jinping orders China's military to be ready for war "at any second"', *South China Morning Post*, 5 January 2021; Yiallourides, C., 'Is China using force or coercion in the South China Sea? Why words matter', *The Diplomat*, 11 July 2018; and Medcalf, *op. cit.*, pp. 175–9.

Chapter 8: Concepts of War

1 It is unlikely that Sun Tzu actually said this, but it fits his overall philosophy well (in this, I agree with Gian P. Gentile in his article 'The accidental coindinista: A historian's journey back from the dark side of Social science,' *Infinity Journal*, October 2012). For a detailed introduction to Sun Tzu's work, see Sun Tzu, *The Art of War*, translated by Samuel B. Griffiths, Oxford University Press, 1963.

2 Molan, J., *Running the War in Iraq*, HarperCollins Publishers, Sydney, 2008.

Chapter 9: Current Policy

1 Morrison, S., 'Launch of the 2020 Defence Strategy Update', *Australian Journal of Defence and Strategic Studies*, Vol.2, No.2, 2020.

2 Morrison, S. and Payne, M., 'Australia to pursue nuclear-powered submarines through new trilateral enhanced security partnership', *Australian Government: Defence*, 16 September 2021.

3 Hartcher, P., 'How Australia has shaped up to Xi's aggression', *Sydney Morning Herald*, 12 October 2021.

4 Curran, J., 'AUKUS is the death knell of Australia's strategic ambiguity', *Defense One*, 20 September 2021.

5   Power, J., 'US should give Australia access to operations in Singapore, Guam, Philippines: Report', *South China Morning Post: This Week in Asia*, 15 October 2021.

6   Bramston, T., 'Defending Taiwan against Beijing is a must, says Peter Dutton', *The Australian*, 12 November 2021.

7   Bramston, *op. cit.*

8   Keating, P., 'Address to the National Press Club of Australia', 10 November 2021.

9   Bramston, *op. cit.*

10   Eckstein, M., 'US Navy reorganizes submarine enterprise to address challenges in construction, maintenance', *Defense News*, 28 September 2021.

11   Greene, A., 'Australian Defence Force may use Collins Class submarines for another 30 years while waiting for nuclear replacements', *ABC News*, 15 October 2021.

12   'Defending Australia in the Asia Pacific century: Force 2030', *Defence White Paper 2009*, Department of Defence, Canberra, 2009.

Chapter 10: The Right War

1   Layton, P., *China's Enduring Grey-zone Challenge*, Air and Space Power Centre, Commonwealth of Australia, Canberra, 2021, p. 46.

2   De Luce, D. and Dilanian, K., 'China's growing firepower casts doubt on whether U.S. could defend Taiwan', *NBC News*, 27 March 2021.

Chapter 11: Can the US Win?

1   Wickman, T., 'COMPACAF focuses on threats, Airmen efforts in Pacific at AFA Warfare Symposium Conference', 4 March 2022.

2   Copp, T., *op. cit.*

3   Davis, M., 'Towards China's A2AD 2.0', *Australian Strategic Policy Institute: The Strategist*, 24 November 2017.

4 Missile Defense Project, 'DF-21 (CSS-5)', *Missile Threat: Center for Strategic and International Studies*, 13 April 2016.

5 Judson, J., 'Iron Dome heads to missile defense experiment in Guam', *Defense News*, 8 October 2021.

6 Axe, D., 'Anticipating war with China, the U.S. Air Force is fanning out across the Pacific', *Forbes*, 7 June 2021.

7 Missile Defense Project, 'Aegis Ashore', *Missile Threat: Center for Strategic and International Studies*, 14 April 2016.

8 Richardson, D.Z., Nahom, D.S. and Guastella, J.T., *Air Force, Force Structure and Modernization Programs: Presentation to the Senate Armed Services Committee Subcommittee on Airland*, US Senate, 22 June 2021.

9 Peck, M., 'U.S. stealth fighter jets are a problem for China – but Beijing says it has the answer', *The National Interest*, 8 July 2021.

10 Del Toro, C., *One Navy–Marine Corps team: Strategic Guidance from the Secretary of the Navy*, October 2021, quoted in Katz, J., 'Navy Secretary's new guidance puts the target on China', *Breaking Defense*, 8 October 2021.

11 Office of the Secretary of Defense, *Military and Security Developments involving the People's Republic of China*, Department of Defense, 2021, pp. 67, 81 and 120–1.

12 China Power Team, 'How is China modernizing its nuclear forces?', *China Power: Center for Strategic and International Studies*, 10 December 2019, updated 28 October 2020.

13 Yoshihara and Holmes, *op. cit.*, p. 150.

14 Batchelor, T., 'U.S. deploys one-third of Pacific submarine fleet for major naval exercise', *Newsweek*, 4 June 2021.

15 Axe, D., 'All three of the U.S. Navy's most powerful submarines were under way at the same time', *Forbes*, 1 August 2021.

16 *Ibid.*

17 Yoshihara and Holmes, *op. cit.*, p. 154.

18 Bowman, B. and Montgomery, M., 'AUKUS: Good goals, bad implementation', *Defense One*, 27 September 2021.

19 'An interactive look at the U.S.–China military scorecard',
    RAND Project Air Force, www.rand.org/paf/projects/us-
    china-scorecard.html.
20 Peniston, B., 'US Navy's latest plan for its future may not come
    until 2023, says top admiral', *Defense One*, 24 September
    2021.
21 'U.S., Philippines: A rocket deal that will make waves in the
    South China Sea', *Stratfor*, 3 April 2019.

Chapter 12: Australia, Defend Yourself!

1   A similar approach has been adopted in the US. As
    commentators have noted: 'The new US *National Defense
    Strategy* that the Biden administration is writing should assess
    core U.S. strategic objectives and delineate the necessary
    Department of Defense capabilities, capacities, and forward
    posture required. This new strategy should be adequately
    resourced, or it will be destined for irrelevance.' See Spoehr,
    Bowman, Clark and Eaglen, *op. cit.*
2   Morrison, S., 'Launch of the 2020 Defence Strategy Update',
    Australian Journal of Defence and Strategic Studies, Vol.2,
    No.2, 2020.

ACKNOWLEDGEMENTS

The impetus for this book was my limited success in convincing people that national security needed more attention. In late 2020, I realised that my challenges were due to a lack of national awareness of the likely nature of any war, much less a regional war involving China. To overcome this deficiency, I decided I would have to describe such a war; this book includes that description.

The period during which I wrote was both personally and nationally tumultuous. Early on, I was diagnosed with an aggressive form of cancer, for which I am still receiving treatment. At the same time, COVID lockdowns were disrupting many lives and livelihoods, and I had to perform most of my senatorial duties remotely. The final stages of the book were completed during the May 2022 election campaign, which of course had an unsuccessful outcome for the Coalition. But the time I spent campaigning, and the many conversations I had with everyday Australians about their priorities and concerns, only served to reinforce the value of completing this work.

I would particularly like to thank the Hon. Peter Dutton MP, the former Coalition Minister for Defence, who not only encouraged me to be outspoken on defence but agreed to write the foreword.

I also thank former prime minister the Hon. Tony Abbott AC and former deputy prime minister the Hon. John Anderson AO for the many discussions we have had and the guidance they have given me.

My gratitude to Mary Rennie, Publisher, Non-Fiction and Commercial Fiction, and Senior Editor Scott Forbes at HarperCollins for guiding me through this often-lonely process, and to David Connery for assistance with local editing.

I also wish to mention my Senate staff, who have provided stellar support during a difficult and highly unusual term of government. While they were not involved in writing this book, we all still argue as to who thought of the title!

But, as always, my deepest and most enduring gratitude is reserved for my wife, Anne. She has supported this project in the same steadfast, wholehearted way she has supported all my professional passions, and has shown more love and endurance than any husband deserves. I could not have survived cancer, much less the process of writing a book alongside my political activities, without her.